29.95

When Good Companies Do Bad Things

When Good Companies Do Bad Things

Responsibility and Risk
in an Age of Globalization

**Peter Schwartz
and Blair Gibb**

John Wiley & Sons, Inc.
New York • Chichester • Weinheim • Brisbane • Singapore • Toronto

Published by John Wiley & Sons, Inc.
Published simultaneously in Canada.

This publication is designed to provide accurate and authoritative information in regard to the subject matter covered. It is sold with the understanding that the publisher is not engaged in rendering professional services. If legal, accounting, medical, psychological or any other expert assistance is required, the services of a competent professional person should be sought.

Library of Congress Cataloging-in-Publication Data:
Schwartz, Peter, 1946-
    When good companies do bad things : responsibility and risk in an age of globalization / Peter Schwartz and Blair Gibb.
        p.   cm.
    Includes bibliographical references and index.
    ISBN 0-471-32332-2 (cloth : alk. paper)
    1. Social responsibility of business.   2. International business enterprises.   I. Gibb, Blair, 1947– .   II. Title.
HD60.S39 1999
658.4'08—dc21   98-31700
                                                                  CIP

Printed in the United States of America.
10 9 8 7 6 5 4 3 2 1

To Ben, Devlin, Emily, Nell, and Kate

Contents

Acknowledgments

Thanking all the people who have helped make this book possible would have been hard enough without the fact that almost everyone to whom we've spoken in the past year has had an opinion (usually thoughtful and interesting) on the subject. Corporate social responsibility is obviously a topic of concern not only to specialists or even only to people in business, but to many others—campaigners, politicians, artists, environmentalists, teenagers, consumers, investors. Indeed, a large part of our argument in this book is that many more people today feel themselves to be stakeholders in corporate decisions than those corporations may realize.

That said, there are still people who warrant special thanks. Three people's conversations (with us and with each other) were the catalysts for the ideas we carried forward: Peter Sutherland, international business executive and former head of the General Agreement on Tariffs & Trade (GATT); Sir Geoffrey Chandler, indefatigable Chair of Amnesty United Kingdom's Business Group; and Pierre Sané, Secretary General of Amnesty International. Colleagues at Global Business Network (GBN) helped enormously with their interest and insights, most especially Napier Collyns, Don Michael, Katherine Fulton, Raimondo Boggia, and Kees Van Der Heijden. Tadashi Nakamae of Nakamae International Economic Research in Tokyo offered exceptional insight into corporate social responsibility issues in Japan. The businesspeople we interviewed, some of whom are quoted in the book and others who are not, spoke of their personal concerns and dilemmas with an honesty and intensity that confirmed for us how timely our topic was. The nongovernmental organization (NGO) campaigners we met reminded us always that behind the apparent abstraction of some of these issues lies a reality in which human lives will be either saved or lost, depending on the outcomes of corporate and societal decisions. And in the end, of course, the support of Diane Taylor and Henning Gutmann of John Wiley & Sons gave our book a reality of its own.

Preface

The issues raised by this book have evolved out of the discipline of traditional business ethics. When coauthor Blair Gibb graduated from Columbia University's Graduate School of Business in 1984, the term "business ethics" was assumed primarily to concern questions of employee relations, procurement practices, corporate policies on acceptance of gifts, and similar narrowly defined operational issues, largely internal and largely defined by legal compliance concerns. At Columbia that year, the topic was covered in a one-hour session in a required "Fundamentals of Business" course, a discussion that generated a fair amount of laughter from the class. The professor's summary: "Don't do anything that you wouldn't want to see on the front page of the *Times*." It was hard then to find nonspecialist books—or even journal articles—on the broader questions of business and its role in society.

In contrast, Columbia today offers students a full-term seminar on "Transnational Business Practices and International Human Rights," covering cases such as Freeport in Indonesia and Royal Dutch/Shell in Nigeria, the conflicts faced by companies doing business in China and Myanmar, and the role of U.S. companies in the international arms trade. The prospect of reading about your company—or yourself—on the front page of the *New York Times* in this context no longer seems as amusing to budding corporate executives as it did in 1984.

When we decided to write this book, it was not out of an interest in looking at the subject of corporate social responsibility through the lens of any particular discipline—theological, financial, psychological, geographic, or political. We wrote this book because we had spent years involved with individual human beings living within large organizations, struggling with these issues in their work lives—Peter Schwartz through his strategic planning experiences with senior executives at multinational corporations, Blair Gibb through her own consulting work and her work with Amnesty International.

We both had an acute sense of the difficulty our colleagues (including ourselves!) faced in sorting out the economic, moral, and practical problems confronting them. We wanted to pull our own experiences and those of others together into a book that might support those individuals and might help change assumptions, policies, and practices that were getting in the way of solutions to those problems. This book is not an academic or theoretical book; it is a book for people who take their responsibility for the future personally and want to make a difference. We believe that description applies to most of the people who work for the corporations whose cases we summarize throughout this book.

Our second reason for writing this book is that corporations have real power in this world (more than they think they have, but less than many citizens think they have). We believe that any organization with power—governments, civic organizations, and corporations—can benefit themselves and others, in the long term, by identifying and acting on opportunities to improve the societies in which they operate. To quote from an interview with Robert Fuller, "what are morals but long-term predictions of social equilibrium?" The instruction from Jesus or the Buddha to do to others what you would have them do unto you, was practical, indeed, Darwinian advice, designed to encourage the kind of behavior that would lead to the long-term success of that very human society from which business is literally inseparable.

Introduction

*Ten years ago we would never have had
human rights on the agenda at this conference.*
—Oil company CEO, Tallberg Conference,
Sweden, June 1998

The title of this book, "When Good Companies Do Bad Things," is meant to raise issues and provoke questions: What does having a good corporate reputation mean in the globalized economy? Who defines what is good and bad corporate behavior, and how are those definitions legitimized? How do companies with good reputations nevertheless find themselves on the firing line of public opinion, and what can they do to prevent such crises? How can the individuals who make up corporations respond to the challenges of creating and sustaining those reputations through their daily operational decisions?

As a number of celebrated cases in recent years have illustrated, these questions are by no means academic or abstract. First and most important, we have seen far too many examples of situations in which company behavior either directly or indirectly resulted in harm, or even death, to innocent human beings. Second, we need to look at such crises from the other side of the glass: When a company finds itself being pilloried by the press and/or its customers, the consequences are real for both the organization and the individuals involved. Here are some incidents drawn from the cases we outline in Chapter 3:

- The CEO of one of the world's largest corporations is warned, before attending his mother's birthday party, that "the neighbors think you're a criminal."

- The recipient of a major media award forces the award sponsor to return the $10,000 that a multinational company has paid for a table at the dinner and says he will not attend if executives from the company are present.
- A 15-year-long class action suit finally ends in the bankruptcy and sale of a multi-billion-dollar manufacturer.

What do these incidents have in common? They all resulted from corporations being blindsided by issues that violated the trust of large segments of the public—their markets. The other feature these incidents have in common is that the individuals within those companies felt their organizations to be *good companies*—until the storm broke.

These companies, like most of the companies discussed in this book, are respected in their industries, highly regarded by their employees, coveted as investors by their communities. One, Royal Dutch/Shell, regularly appears near the top of *Fortune* magazine's list of most admired companies. These companies do not intentionally cut corners on safety, make fraudulent product claims, evade legislative controls, or violate employment laws. Assuredly, too many companies in the world do commit such violations and some are described in this book, but there are legal mechanisms to deal with their activities, and by and large such companies do not enjoy widespread public respect to begin with. Our concern is with those companies who had that respect, lost it, and had to begin the long struggle to regain it. What went wrong? Could they have avoided their crises? Have companies become less ethical, or have society's standards changed? What will companies have to do differently in the future to avoid similar fates? And finally, what must the business community as a whole learn from these examples?

1

Social Responsibility in the Context of Globalization

Cooperate with those who have both know-how and integrity.
—FORTUNE COOKIE, JAPANESE TEA GARDEN, SAN FRANCISCO (APRIL 14, 1998)

This book is about the strategic relationship between know-how and integrity and about the fact that a company cannot be successful in the long term without both. In this context, the deeper meanings of the word "integrity" require exploration. As Grand Metropolitan's first *Report on Corporate Citizenship* (1997) states:

> Integrity has two meanings. First, it is the quality of being honest, upright, ethical and uncompromising about values and principles.
>
> But integrity also means the quality of being integrated. This second meaning is also a vital part of what GrandMet is and aspires to be. In addition to being honest, upright and ethical, we want to be understood as both consistent and in tune with the societies and communities in which we live and make our living.

We believe that the concept of social responsibility has begun to move, in response to globalization, beyond the first definition of in-

1

tegrity (reflecting the earlier concerns with business ethics) and toward the second. A variety of forces—geopolitical, economic, and
demographic—have been driving this process and contributing to
the public's changing expectations of business.

Chang-ing view of business

One of the first significant influences, although business by and
large did not recognize it as such, was the signing of the Universal
Declaration of Human Rights in 1948. This document, created by
the members of the new United Nations in the wake of World War
II, moved the concept of international law well beyond traditional
maritime and trade concerns and into the less mapped territory of
civil, political, economic, social, and cultural rights. It established for
the first time a measure of international consensus on these core
rights of citizens. Its preamble, as well, clearly stated that protection
of these rights was the duty of all societal institutions, not just governments. The implications of this statement have become more
contentious in the 50 years since, with the apartheid era in South
Africa producing the first major collision between heightened democratic expectations of the world's peoples and the practice of "business as usual." Companies were asked by antiapartheid campaigners
to make major investment and disinvestment decisions on moral
grounds; those decisions were not simple, and their results are still
being debated today.

Even during the so-called Me Decade of the 1980s, social issues
were becoming more visible on corporate radars (the British organization Business in the Community, for example, was founded in
1982). From 1989 onward, the process accelerated, partially because
of the collapse of the socialist economies—but the driving forces
were not all political. The economics of globalization, and the creation of a worldwide market for the first time in a century, led commentators to start treating "capitalism" and "democracy" as twinned
values. The western economic model seemed destined to claim all of
Asia, Africa, and Latin America, with American and European
transnational corporations (TNCs) playing modern versions of
Christopher Columbus, Vasco da Gama, Hernando Cortés, John
Cabot, and Jacques Cartier. As these corporations surged into what
had been closed markets and non-European social systems, questions
began to arise about how those corporations, and the financial institutions that supported them, would use their power.

The year 1995 then proved to be a flash point, as Royal Dutch/Shell found itself grappling publicly with two explosive issues: the environment and human rights (Brent Spar and Nigeria). Also in 1995 *When Corporations Rule the World* was published, a book that declared: "once beneficial corporations and financial institutions [have been transformed] into instruments of a market tyranny that is extending its reach across the planet like a cancer, colonizing ever more of the planet's living spaces, destroying livelihoods, displacing people, rendering democratic institutions impotent, and feeding on life in an insatiable quest for money."

These kinds of accusations clearly go well beyond the old business ethics case studies and into the deepest questions a society can ask itself. The wave of books that have been addressing "business and social responsibility" for the past decade therefore examines the subject from a refreshingly wide variety of angles: philosophical, religious, academic, even economic.

Despite the significance of these recent developments, it is important to remember that the role played by public opinion in shaping corporate behavior is not new. There are lessons to be learned as well from earlier periods in which companies, indeed entire industries, had to change or die in response to criticism, as we discuss in Chapter 2. The effects of globalization, however, have changed dramatically both the nature of that criticism and its targets. According to the United Nations, in 1975 there were 7,000 transnational corporations; in 1994, there were 37,000. Globalization has changed not only industry structures, but communications networks and markets as well. Business behavior may have had worldwide impact in the eighteenth and nineteenth centuries and even before then (witness the East India Tea Company), but information about those effects, and the public's ability to react, now reaches worldwide audiences also.

One annoying aspect of the term *globalization* is that while thousands of people use it, few define it precisely, thus leaving the rest of us unsure whether we are discussing the same thing. In our view, the term "globalization" does not refer to one single process, but serves as shorthand for several related processes. In Sweden, at the 1990 Tallberg conference on globalization and business responsibility, executives in a working group suggested the following phenomena as comprising globalization:

- An increasingly shared awareness across many publics
- A new, international financial web
- New open space into which dominating cultures can move
- Progress from "inter-national" to global institutions
- Declining importance of geography
- Dangerous new linkages possible
- Greater speed of events
- Trend away from nation-states and toward regions or "tribes"

By defining globalization in this way, it is possible to see clearly how each of these developments has helped broaden society's expectations of business and its social responsibility. "Shared awareness across publics" means that civic or voluntary organizations can now represent many millions, rather than hundreds, of consumers or voters and that the new international media can mobilize those millions overnight if it chooses. The new "financial web" means that transparency, probity, and rule of law are more important, to more people, than ever—violators of these principles can bring large segments of the entire network down (witness the Asian crisis). The "open space" for dominating cultures means more and deeper debate over values as those cultures collide with others who, reasonably, feel their very existence to be threatened. The creation of global, as opposed to "inter-national," institutions means a transitional period during which old institutions will appear increasingly ineffective and new ones (like multinationals) represent an unknown force. "Declining importance of geography" means that people all over the world can consider themselves stakeholders in decisions made by businesses anywhere. "Dangerous new linkages" refers to any number of emerging networks—technological, criminal, financial—whose impacts the public rightly feels unsure of, and over which they feel less and less control. The "greater speed" at which the world now operates means that a company whose intelligence networks break down or that becomes insulated from its markets or communities can be blindsided by changing attitudes more quickly than ever. Finally, the shift of power away from nation-states means that the public in general requires more accountability from other powerful actors, such as business, and expects them to respond directly to the demands of public opinion rather than waiting for that opinion to be mediated by government in the form of legislation or regulation.

Each of these aspects of globalization, then, represents another dynamic pushing companies toward a broader interpretation of their obligations to society. It was easy for many companies not to perceive this development at first, especially in the wake of the apparent collapse of socialist ethics around the world. For most market liberals, that collapse was a long-overdue response to communist regimes' distortion of basic economic principles in the service of political or social goals. The collapse was therefore at first perceived by business leaders as a signal that these goals themselves were less legitimate or valid—that the market alone could and should be allowed to solve every human problem. Talk of social responsibility, especially if it came from trade unions seeking to impose western labor standards on signatories to international trade agreements, struck many of those leaders as dangerous backsliding toward the regulated, inefficient and politically driven economies of social planners.

This apparent conflict between efficiency and equity has produced a wide range of proposed solutions, ranging from extreme libertarianism to unreconstructed advocacy of public ownership of the means of production. Most of us fall somewhere within the broad middle, seeking a balance of cost and benefit that works both for our own enterprises and for society as a whole. The discrediting of the state socialist model did not, as many thought it would, answer the question of how to find that balance—it reopened the question on different terms.

The other worldwide phenomenon that has triggered new societal demands on business is closely related to globalization: the privatization process that has advanced almost as quickly. Countries that once thought only governments could operate (for example) airports, seaports, railroads, and public utilities are rushing to turn these functions over to the private sector. Figure 1.1 illustrates clearly the scale and parallel development of the two processes in one of the most important developing economies: China. In the United States, privatization of apparently core government functions like criminal justice and education has become a subject of experiment, and as will be noted later, in countries such as Russia, even public safety has been de facto privatized.

The trend toward privatization has led, in turn, to further blurring of the line between business and government. The implications of these overlapping responsibilities are far-reaching and not yet

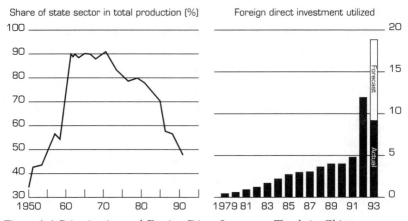

Figure 1.1 Privatization and Foreign Direct Investment Trends in China
Source: *The China Analyst,* Vol. 1.1, BCA Publications, 1993.

clearly understood. If voters are no longer the ultimate source of accountability for privatized functions, who is? Should shareholders of companies exercising formerly public functions have different expectations in terms of return than do shareholders of other types of companies?

Privatization and globalization have therefore imposed dramatic changes on both public and private sectors and have raised issues of balance between competing interests and stakeholders. Along the spectrum of possibility lies a wide range of choices, and it will fall to business to make many of those decisions. The evidence is accumulating, as this book demonstrates, that public opinion is increasingly pushing those choices away from the pure free-market extreme (which never, in actuality, operates without some form of societal restraint anyway). That demand on the part of the public, the search for a proper balance, is at the heart of the call for corporate social responsibility.

The environmental movement exemplifies the evolution of the conflict. Here is how one CEO described the process of coming to terms with environmentalism: "Thirty years ago we objected; twenty years ago we started to accept it; ten years ago we started to move." One way of explaining the change is to assume that companies simply gave in to the growing power of public concern for the environment, without any real change in belief systems. In some cases this explanation may be true; but in others, it seems clear that perceptions have genuinely changed and that business has come to see that destructive environmental policies, even if they appear efficient and cost-effective in the short run, are literally not sustainable in the long run. According to some executives, other issues of social responsibility (such as human rights, for example) are now at the beginning stages of the same process.

Environmentalism set the terms of this discourse in a more basic way by diffusing systems thinking throughout broad populations. Thirty years ago, environmental organizations had to work hard to convince most people that the health of their gardens in Provence or Australia could be affected by damage to rain forests in Brazil or ozone layers in Antarctica. Now these connections are understood by millions on a very intuitive level, and their importance is reinforced by people's ability to observe the power and reach of the financial, technological, and economic networks that globalization has created. More people than ever feel affected, actually or potentially, by decisions made by corporations, and they are in a better position than ever to act on those feelings.

This chapter lists some reasons why the notion of business ethics—which was essentially driven by nationally based legal and regulatory systems—has given way to a broader discussion of social responsibility. Companies that became global or transnational while still operating within ethical systems aimed at complying with purely national standards and at avoiding illegal behavior have found themselves, simply put, playing on the wrong fields by the wrong rules.

2
Business as Villain: A Historical Overview

When public opinion turns against a company or an industry sector, the risk to the core business may range from negligible (a bit of bad press) to terminal (bankruptcy or some form of exiting the business). In the worst of all cases, the impact includes real fatalities—human lives lost, with accusations of corporate responsibility for those losses. In the next chapter, we discuss examples that have caused damage to contemporary companies and examine the limitations of existing risk management strategies in preventing or limiting that damage. At the core of any assessment, however, whatever the degree, lies the concept of reputation—an idea whose importance has survived intact even as its visible manifestations have greatly changed.

Because this chapter is intended to provide a historical context for the rest of the book, a prototype from the past is worth considering—the beginnings of what we now think of as exchanges, the trade-based coffeehouses of the sixteenth and seventeenth centuries. These small-scale meeting places were crucial to the development of today's markets, providing as they did an occasion for participants in a particular trade to do business with one another, seek financing, and otherwise keep track of developments in their field.

An important characteristic of these markets-in-formation was that participants were assumed to be dealing with one another in good faith. Before the days of rating agencies, the business press, government regulations, or other watchdogs, there was a simple and immediate punishment for those who went back on their word, failed to honor commitments, or otherwise did not observe the norms. They were no longer admitted to the exchange and therefore by implication were consigned to the fringes of their industry. In the days when the Baltic Exchange was first active in London, for example, a ship broker would think twice before doing anything that would prevent him from having access to the floor of the exchange, where 90 percent of London ship brokerage was conducted. (As a side note, the initial meaning of the word *boycott* was actually social ostracism—practiced in the nineteenth century by members of the Irish Land League against an English landlord's agent, the unfortunate Colonel Charles Boycott.) Having and maintaining a good reputation, in this context, was literally a matter of company survival.

In all visible aspects, the operating environment of most businesses today might as well be located on another planet from these early exchanges, but the importance of reputation remains. It is a much more generalized concept today; traders may number in the millions and most of them never meet except in cyberspace, but *Fortune's* annual list of companies most admired by their peers is still considered a corporate honor roll whose underlying dynamic is the same as it was in the coffeehouses 300 years ago:

1. Good reputation is a company asset.
2. Good reputations are built up over years and take years to repair, but can be destroyed overnight.

Corporate reputation is an asset because it is linked to brand equity, contributing to the value of the company in ways that may not always be directly quantifiable but are nonetheless real. The Italian strategist Raimondo Boggia, of Alchera Strategic Vision, has described three ways in which the two may interact:

1. The Mitsubishi strategy, where the corporate name and its brands are the same.
2. The Procter and Gamble strategy, where there is no obvious link between the corporate name and its various brands.
3. The Nestlé-style endorsement strategy, where a brand like Nescafé is sold with the implicit or explicit endorsement of the Nestlé corporate name behind it.

Boggia proposes that in the past, the corporate name (connected directly to company reputation) and brand equity (connected to consumer value of a particular product) could be kept separate, but now the two are merging. Why? Boggia's thesis is that as traditional *agencia di socializione* (roughly, "socializing agents") like the church, family, and schools experience dramatic change and become less authoritative educators of the next generations, the media—including corporate advertising—become more important as arbiters of value. Consumers have begun to look to the brand for more than an indicator of product quality—they have begun to look to the brand for reassurance, for broader value, for a way to judge and express their own views of right and wrong.

The implication of this development for companies goes back to our initial discussion of integrity—to use Boggia's words, "Building brand equity is no longer as it was in the 1950s and 1960s, a matter of 'make-up.' The game of advertising is over. It is now about communicating what you really are in an intelligent way." In this world, companies are punished as much for being hypocrites—for behaving inconsistently with their public claims—as for the behavior itself. So although at the moment green and socially oriented consumers may amount to only an average 10 percent of the market, many more people make at least some of their purchasing and shareholding decisions on the basis of company reputation.

The cases we discuss in detail in Chapter 3 demonstrate a variety of ways in which damage to a company's reputation can occur—and the wide range of consequences that can flow from such self-inflicted wounds. Public anger against Royal Dutch/Shell, Unocal, Nike, Nestlé, Texaco, Union Carbide, and other highly respected companies has had long-term as well as short-term impacts, inside the firms as well as outside. As we also note, the influence of modern communications media has played a major role in each of these cases—but long before CNN, or even television, the public's relationship with industrial capitalism and its agents was a stormy one.

This chapter provides a few quick flashbacks to periods of similar antibusiness outrage, when citizens took it upon themselves to change the rules of the business environment. This review is intended to help us learn what we can from history and to remind us that current social issues are often reshaped expressions of concerns that have endured for many years.

The examples that follow date from the beginning of the Industrial Revolution, and while each refers to a different trade or industry, certain common patterns appear. In all of them, an important business activity makes a transition in the eyes of the public from acceptable to unacceptable. These transitions generally occur over a period of years, beginning with certain, almost unnoticed, early indicators and gathering speed when the practice or activity reaches a certain level of visibility, whether because of concentration of power, the position of its advocates, or other, similar factors. Over time, public opinion gradually forces some outside power (in these cases, national governments) to, in turn, force business to change by imposing legal or regulatory constraints. In some cases, such as slave trade and slavery, the business itself ends by being outlawed. In other cases, the business carries on, but is regulated, limited, controlled. With new technological and market innovations, the cycle then begins again.

These large-scale patterns in the public's view of business practices are what our examples highlight. There have been scandals connected with individual companies or entrepreneurs, and there has been plenty of out-and-out-theft, of course, probably since the first consumer in a village market noticed a merchant's thumb being pressed a little too firmly onto the scale. Our examples do not deal with these kinds of ethical problems. Instead, our examples explore the expectations and models of business behavior that society as a whole is developing in order to understand the responsibilities that companies need to assume in the future.

A contemporary instance of this long-term dynamic is the battle over cigarette smoking. Tobacco was first used in pipes by Native Americans, who considered it medicinal. The practice was taken up by Europeans in the mid-sixteenth century, making tobacco the largest crop of the new American colonies. Smoking became widespread in the form of cigarettes after the invention of the cigarette-making machine in the United States in the 1880s. In the 1930s, medical reports linking tobacco smoking to cancer began to surface, but it was not until 1952 that the first mass-media article about the danger appeared (in *Reader's Digest*).

By 1954, the tobacco industry had formed the Tobacco Industry Research Council and began marketing filtered and low-tar cigarettes. The first government warning on the subject came from the Surgeon General's office in 1964. Over the past three decades, the

(text continues on page 19)

1783–1807: The English and American Slave Trade

It is slightly more than 200 years ago in the explosively growing port city of Liverpool, England. One hundred thirty-eight ships—1 out of 12 that left the docks—have sailed in the past year for Africa, carrying British manufactured products for trade there. Thousands of men, women, and children in the Manchester area alone are employed in producing these goods (textiles, household utensils, guns) destined to be exchanged for slaves on the African coast, now that the supply of white indentured servants has proven insufficient to meet the agricultural labor needs of England's new colonies. To complete what is known as the "triangular trade," those ships will then travel on to the West Indies and the mainland American colonies, exchange their human cargo for agricultural and other raw materials, and return again to England to supply its manufacturers with the resources they need to carry on the processes of the Industrial Revolution. Bristol and Glasgow are the two other cities whose enormous population growth, as the eighteenth century draws to a close, is attributed to the trade "which custom immemorial, and various Acts of Parliament, have ratified and given sanction to."

Also by the end of the eighteenth century, Britain's North American colonies, which originally treated the Africans largely the same as European indentured servents, have installed new laws that effectively remove legal personhood from this particular class of persons.

During this period, "the monarchy, the church, the government and public opinion in general" support the slave trade. Few protests are lodged, and those few are largely ineffective (as in the refusal of one William Rathbone to supply timber for construction of slave ships). The slave traders are pillars of English society—mayors, sheriffs bankers, merchants. David Barclay (a Quaker whose fortune will shortly form the basis of Barclay's Bank) is not only a successful trader but the owner of thousands of slaves in Jamaica—whom he will, to his credit, free before the end of the century.

It is only with the revolt of the American colonies and the subsequent change in trading patterns that we find attitudes toward the slave trade beginning to change (Significantly, Thomas

(continued)

Jefferson's first draft of the Declaration of Independence contains an antislavery clause. It is voted out of the final version, but Jefferson stubbornly continues to include it in every copy he circulates afterward.) Abolitionist arguments are easier for the English to stomach once Britain has no monopoly on slave-grown products to defend. "The groans of the sons and daughters of Africa" have suddenly become audible, and William Wilberforce begins his long parliamentary campaign to end the slave trade.

It is by no means an easy fight. The Methodists are the first religious group to take up the cause seriously but are called by one Manchester workers' representative "the vilest crew God ever suffered to infest the earth." Lord North, Prime Minister, congratulates Quaker abolitionists on their humanity, but states that doing as they ask is "impossible." Leading citizens still constitute the backbone of proslavery societies.

After the turn of the century, however, the antislavery position benefits from becoming linked with opposition to the monopolies and with highly visible wealth accumulated by the West Indian planter families, who often use that wealth to buy Parliamentary seats and otherwise offend the sensibilities of the public. As one writer states, "the public would be ... a gainer if estates in the West Indies were so moderate that not a tenth of the West Indian gentlemen who now sit in the House of Commons could obtain that frequently expensive honour."

Having succeeded in outlawing the trade (1807), public opinion then turns on the underlying evil, the slave system itself. The Anti-Slavery Society's object is now to "obtain the free right for the Negroes to possess their own flesh and blood," and public consensus is changing. By 1827, members of Parliament are almost as afraid to speak out in support of slavery as they were 30 years ago to speak out against it. A drunken actor on stage in Liverpool complains that he has "not come here to be offended by a set of wretches ... whose infernal town is cemented with African blood." Slavery itself is finally outlawed in Britain in 1833, 26 years after the banning of the trade.

It is a measure of the continuing power of the West Indian commercial interests however, that it takes even longer—13 years after abolition, in 1846—for English lawmakers to equalize sugar duties and remove the West Indian planters' final protection from competing producers in Asia. It is a measure of the continuing power of the advocates of slave labor that it takes more than another 10 years—and thousands of lives lost in a bloody Civil War—for slavery to be abolished in the United States and another 60 years after that for the world's nations to sign the first international Anti-Slavery Convention.

1869–1877: The Railroad Barons— From Golden Spike to the Great Strikes

It is May 10, 1869—a day of national celebration in the United States. The driving of a ceremonial golden spike at Promontory Point, Utah, marks the completion of the United States' first transcontinental railroad line and sets off parades, fireworks, and political speeches across the country. The completion of the second link, 14 years later in Montana, is stage-managed by the company owner to generate even more excitement, in what historian Page Smith has called a "protracted celebration of American technical accomplishment." Despite the devastating impact that the coming of the railroads has had on Native Americans, even local tribes are caught up in the general excitement, with Chief Sitting Bull joining journalist Carl Schurz in laying the cornerstone of the North Dakota state capitol when the line reaches Bismarck. Cheering crowds, anticipating boom times to come, wave along the path of the dignitaries' private cars as they travel the new line.

The euphoria, unfortunately, does not last—for a reason that signals the profound changes to come, changes that the railroad itself has brought about. Thanks to the massive publicity, investors finally have a chance to see with their own eyes the undeveloped state of the territories through which the new railroad passes and to learn as well the cost of the self-promoting celebrations organized by its management. Investors rush to sell out, the Northern Pacific's holding company goes bankrupt, and demonstrators picket the owner's New York mansion.

In future terminology, we would say that this particular railroad enterprise helped to create the very market information, or transparency, that brought it down—but at this point, such tem-

(continued)

porary setbacks cannot prevent the early railroad barons from achieving enormous power and wealth. By the 1880s, America boasts more railroad track than the rest of the world's countries combined. Andrew Carnegie creates his own fortune mainly by supplying the iron and steel that the new, fast-growing network requires and initially earns himself a reputation as one of the most enlightened of the new industrialists, building model communities for his steel company workers and granting them the eight-hour day before it became law.

These railroad riches lead to enormous growth in other sectors—the so-called robber barons are not only railroad men, but timber, steel mining, and coal men. The demand for low-wage labor seems endless, and the railroads themselves are the nation's largest employer by 1890.

In the meantime, however, the country's mood has turned to something less celebratory. Sympathies begin to shift away from the figurative robbers and toward the real ones: Frank and Jesse James and the Younger gang become almost folk heroes in contrast with the bankers and railroaders whose strongboxes they target. Coleman Younger, once released from prison, becomes a star attraction in the Frank James Wild West Show.

"Wild West Show" could easily be the title of an entire book about this period of railroad history: the dramatic expansions and opening up of territory, the frantic bidding of small towns against each other for the spur lines they thought would guarantee prosperity, the insolvencies of dozens of would be barons, the larger-than-life figures cut by the industry's tycoons (in stark contrast to the images of poverty, injury, and death that attach to their largely immigrant workforce).

The new industrial stars—George Pullman, George Westinghouse, Andrew Carnegie, Henry Frick, John D. Rockefeller, and others—thus move to the center of the American stage against a backdrop of increasing economic depression and despair. When these long-held grievances erupt in violence, it is directed first and foremost against the railroads. The Baltimore & Ohio announces in July of 1877 that workers' pay will be reduced by an average of more than 10 percent, bringing firemen, some of the highest paid employees, down to $1.58 per day. Workers begin to walk off the job, in small groups at first. By the end of the month, the strike has spread from railroad workers to canal men, box makers, and almost every other type of labor required to move freight.

Over the next few weeks, not only Baltimore but Trenton, Newark, Philadelphia, Reading, Pittsburgh, Columbus, Chicago, St. Louis, Scranton, Syracuse, Albany, Buffalo, and San Francisco all explode in outbreaks of mass rioting, by women and children as well as workmen. By the end of what will come to be called the Great Strikes, there have been hundreds killed, thousands wounded, and hundreds of millions of dollars in property damage done, primarily to the railroads themselves—the bringers of prosperity, the symbols of "man's power and skill and success." The strikes also leave mirror-imaged political legacies that will not only live on but thrive into the twentieth century: a strong anti-communism among the governing classes and heightened political consciousness on the part of labor.

A significant portion of the public is in sympathy with the strikers. The *Chicago Daily News* stated: "For years the railroads of this country have been run outside the United States Constitution...they have corrupted Congress...finally, having found nothing more to get out of the stockholders, they have commenced raiding upon not only the general public but their own employees."

In the aftermath of the strikes, some industry members institute important reforms the Baltimore & Ohio creates the Relief Association to assist the families of injured workers and four years later sets up a company pension plan. Labor agitation and organization grow stronger: Ten years after the Great Strikes, there are 1,411 strikes in one year, involving 2,928 companies and half a million workers.

As for Andrew Carnegie, the Scottish author of *Triumphant Democracy*, whose motto was "Death to Privilege," the 1892 strike at his Homestead steel mill results in armed warfare between workers and hired security forces. Afterward, an English newspaper pronounces Carnegie's book on democracy "a wholesome piece of satire," and the *St. Louis Post-Dispatch* concludes, "Three months ago Andrew Carnegie was a man to be envied. Today he is an object of mingled pity and contempt...ten thousand

(continued)

'Carnegie Public Libraries' would not compensate the country for the evils resulting from Homestead."

1890–1960: The Imperial Corporation

As the slavery example illustrates, the development of foreign colonies by European nations had mercantilism at its heart. New markets, and new sources of raw materials, were needed by the industrializing economies of England, France, Spain, Portugal, and Holland. As the nineteenth century ends, mercantilism has assumed new forms, but the result looks much the same: corporate expansion backed by state power. The agony of its Civil War ended and its own western frontier pushing against the Pacific, the new United States of America is joining the game with enthusiasm.

One of the most straightforward examples of corporate colonization is the 1892 annexation of Hawaii. The initial European settlers, mostly Christian missionaries, quickly move into less spiritual pursuits—the original Castle and Cooke, who in 1851 form what will become one of the world's largest food companies, arrived in the islands as missionaries only 14 years before. By the 1890s, these interests have formed an Annexation Committee seeking incorporation into the United States, and in 1893, at the request of the committee, 160 Marines land in Honolulu and occupy the capital, overthrowing Queen Lili'uokalani. The self-declared first president of Hawaii's Provisional Government? President Dole.

Over the next several decades, few fruit tycoons actually go this far to ensure protection of their commercial interests, but in countries such as the Philippines, Guatemala, Honduras, Nicaragua, the West Indies and Cuba, they certainly do assist in the installation of friendly governments, sometimes by force. The term "banana republic," originating from the activities of companies like United Fruit, is invented to describe these puppet regimes. Some of the most famous Americans in Central America at the turn of the century are referred to as "banana men," especially Sam Zemurray, who bankrolled the Honduran "revolution" of 1910–11, won a 10,000-hectare plantation in result, and eventually came to run the United Fruit Company. These and other exploits around the world lead to the formation of organizations such as the Anti-Imperialist League and to campaign denunciations of imperialist adventures.

International labor unions and socialist movements integrate battles against neocolonialism into their battles against capitalists at home. Later, despite events such as the CIA's 1954 invasion of Guatemala and the violent end of the Salvador Allende regime in Chile, a major theme of the middle twentieth century becomes the resistance of former colonies to the continued influence of foreign capital. Entire theories of development—import substitution, aggressive industrialization often coupled with nationalization and confiscation of foreign assets—grow up around this resistance.

Finally, well into the 1980s, legal and political barriers to foreign investment begin to fall in many countries. However, disputes about the appropriate role of international corporations in the developing world continue even as the process of globalization accelerates: disputes in the policy arena (as in negotiations over the Multilateral Agreement on Investment and in the ongoing, modern versions of earlier labor disputes (Iris fruit multinational Fyffes and its Belize operations, Chiquita in Honduras, tobacco and coffee growers in Central America).

laws in this area have changed dramatically in the United States, and cigarette manufacturers are being held to a stricter liability standard.

Today, public attitudes in the United States are increasingly, and often stridently, antismoking as new medical information on smoking's dangers becomes available. Although this change has not yet taken place in the rest of the world, there is a good chance, given the pattern we have identified in our examples, that it will—and that a multi-billion-dollar industry will eventually disappear after a run of more than 400 years.

Although the histories in our examples focus on European and American companies, the dynamics apply more broadly. The past 40 years, for example, have also seen a profound rethinking in Japan about the role of companies there.

The first, and in some ways most violent, corporate shock of Japan's postwar reconstruction period was the environmental disaster at the small town of Minamata. Minamata had persuaded the Chisso

Corporation to locate there in 1907 to provide jobs for a population that otherwise subsisted almost entirely on fishing. By 1925, the company was dumping waste into Minamata Bay and the fishing areas were beginning to be damaged. In response to complaints, Chisso decided to make compensation payments to villages who protested rather than change its processes. This practice continued until the mid 1950s, when local residents began developing a disease that later came to be known as "Minamata Disease"; mercury poisoning. Victims' nervous systems degenerated; some people lapsed into comas while others began behaving as if deranged. Domestic animals began committing suicide, and birds began to drop from the sky. In 1956, a Chisso chemist blamed the disease on the population's diet of fish from Minamata Bay, but the company denied that they were responsible and continued dumping waste in the area.

Finally, in July 1959, independent researchers determined that the Chisso Corporation's mercury discharges were the cause of the disease. Dr. Hosokawa, the Chisso chemist, tried in secret to demonstrate the truth of this accusation to company management, but he was banned from conducting further experiments and his findings were concealed. (In a sad postscript, Dr. Hosokawa told the entire story just before he died, after suffering internal torments for years but feeling that loyalty to his company prevented him from telling his story until then. His deathbed testimony proved crucial to the Japanese court's final verdict in 1973.)

The Minamata case eventually became a symbol—not only "of the costs of high growth, but of a new type of citizen activism in Japan." The Minamata fishermen were weak and isolated victims when they began protesting in 1959. It was not until 1968, when their protests had gathered momentum and when photographs of suffering victims and their deformed children began horrifying the entire nation, that Chisso finally stopped dumping poison into the region's waters. The Japanese government itself became involved, lending the corporation money to make compensation payments and trying to prevent the company from going broke.

In 1973 the company was found guilty of "the liability of negligence," according to the Kumamoto District Court. The 40-year-old case was finally settled in October 1995 with an agreement that the government would relax its standards for determining who qualified as victims, that the government would express its regret for the role it played in the disaster, and that the defendant company would pay the equivalent of $26,000 each to the remaining uncompensated victims.

Around the time of the first court ruling in the Minamata case, the Japanese public was suffering from the effects of the first oil shock (1973–1974). This shock resulted in another corporate scandal: the discovery that trading companies and refineries in Japan were, in the public's eyes, hoarding low-cost oil and trying to gouge the public by charging new, higher prices for it. The companies claimed that they were only trying to smooth out the distribution system in time-honored fashion, but the argument was not persuasive to the general public.

The recent (1995–1998) financial scandals involving brokerages and financial institutions have brought further changes in the Japanese people's traditional respect for the business community. The close personal relationships between stockbrokers and Ministry of Finance officials—in the course of which many ministry officials benefited from gifts and other perquisites—have turned from business as usual into criminal acts. In April 1998, the Japanese finance minister announced that 112 officials would be punished for accepting excessive entertainment from financial entities under their supervision, for allegedly alerting banks to the timing of government audits, and for favoring certain firms in authorizing new financial products. More than 1,000 officials were investigated by the ministry, and several of them resigned rather than face prosecution or internal disciplinary procedures.

Another dramatic example of these changes in public attitudes is the crisis at Nomura Securities. In 1997, 20 of the company's directors were forced to resign and several executives were arrested for bribery. Daiwa Securities, Dai-Ichi Kangyo Bank, and Yamaichi Securities, all major firms, were also implicated in the scandal. In the words of *The Economist,* "bad enough for Nomura, but far worse was the damage done to an already tarnished industry. The Nomura affair confirmed that crooks, the rich and the powerful (and often a combination of all three) make money from the stockmarket...all of them clearly continue to think that individual investors are fair game."

These revelations have caused major shifts in public opinion even within a culture as resistant to conflict as Japan's and testify to the power of the rising standards increasingly being applied to business behavior worldwide. These examples confirm that corporations as social organizations have been the targets of various reform movements throughout history. The experiences summarized in this chapter underscore this fact: Each concentration of power seems to hold within itself the germ of its own opposition. As soon as power becomes too visible, too proud, too concentrated, a movement of some kind sets out to limit or constrain it.

This cycle holds true in each of our boxed examples. The international system of slavery was eventually eliminated, surviving largely in the form of sex workers, prison, or forced labor in economic backwaters. The railroads were first prosecuted, later regulated, and finally broken up (only to be reunited again in new forms as vertically integrated parts of logistics companies). Company practices that governments first endorsed and encouraged metamorphosed into criminal behavior in the face of public opposition. Exploitative foreign Multinational Corporations (MNCs) were first nationalized, were then subjected to discriminatory foreign investment rules, and are now increasingly accepted as partners by developing country governments as long as they play by the new rules.

The lessons for business still apply: With concentration of power (resulting either from innovation, cost position, or market control) come domination and visibility, especially in a world in which companies have worldwide presence. A company may, surprisingly, be unaware of how large a target it has come to represent, despite the fact that domination and visibility are inextricably connected today. The result is inevitable public demands for accountability and transparency—demands that in the past have been enforced by the legislative and regulatory powers of national governments. Such originally radical proposals as the legal humanity of African Americans, an eight-hour workday, publicly funded education, prohibitions on child labor, and women's right to vote have, of course, generally taken decades to become law. Given the extent to which commercial interests seemed able to control the political process itself, reformers of the past may have felt that governmental powers were very slender reeds on which to hang the hope of bringing those commercial interests under control.

Today, those slender reeds, compared to any individual government's current ability to constrain the typical transnational corporation, look like redwoods. This new factor—globalization, as we noted earlier, is the shorthand for it—has led to higher levels of anxiety on the part of a public confronted with modern concentrations of market power (see books like Korten's *When Corporations Rule the World*). Who, today, can effectively regulate an oil company active in 160 countries? a clothing manufacturer with factories in 50 countries? What governments today would even try? Instead, they seem intent on eliminating what vestigial regulation they do practice in order to be more attractive to foreign investors who provide their constituents with jobs. And would the old style of regulation even work under the new order?

It is because nobody can easily imagine the answers to these questions that the issue of corporate social responsibility has become so disputatious. As governments withdraw from norm-setting activity, a civic empty space has been created into which business seems free to flow as it wishes. To its surprise, however, business has found a new type of organization occupying this empty space: the international NGO (nongovernmental organization, a clumsy description, but significant in the sense that it implies people are more sure of what this new creature is not, than of what it is). These NGOs are the Greenpeaces, Amnesty Internationals, Oxfams, and Red Cross/Red Crescents of the world, and while they are definitely not governments, they seem to be playing more of the role that governments once did, especially when they catch the eye of the international media. Are these NGOs the forces, then, that will play the role necessary to keep this historical cycle of innovation–concentration–domination/visibility–constraint/reform moving in a positive direction? Keep in mind this key question during the next chapter, as we explore contemporary examples of corporate battles with public opinion.

3

Corporations Today

*We strive to be good corporate citizens
but we sometimes make mistakes.*
—Royal Dutch/Shell, The Shell Report,
Profits and Principles—Does There Have
to Be a Choice? 1998

In this chapter we take up examples from recent years that illustrate the new environment adapted by the cycle described in the previous chapter. Although we could have cited many cases, the ones in this chapter were chosen for a few key reasons.

1. Most of the companies highlighted in this chapter have been the subject of extensive press coverage and have therefore undergone the sort of trial by fire that brings issues most sharply into focus.
2. These cases represent a range of issues with which advocates of social responsibility are concerned: the environment, human rights, health and safety, gender and racial equity, labor standards, and transparency.
3. These examples include companies from a range of industries— resource extraction, manufacturing, fashion, and food.
4. Company responses to each crisis also represent a range of possible actions: development of new international agreements and/or standards; development of new internal policies and/or practices; continuation of existing practice in the face of criticism. That the cases are, on the surface, very different in their circumstances and outcomes makes the commonalities that we explore later all the more interesting.

We use a key tool to provide a context for our analysis: the "business idea." Readers who are familiar with Kees van der Heijden's book and GBN scenario development work will know the concept of the business idea behind any successful company. Readers who are encountering this concept for the first time might think it means simply to make money, as when people say that corporations exist only to make a profit. Making money is not a business idea. The business idea refers to a firm's essential concept of itself, its distinctive competencies. Any organization, commercial or noncommercial, generally has such a concept at the heart of what it does. For example, part of the business idea of many resource companies is a picture of themselves as the "partner of choice" for country governments wishing to develop their natural mining or energy resources. With this business idea, reputation and image—and following through on long-term commitments— become an important part of a company's commercial success strategy. The Shell case in this chapter is an example of this approach.

The notion of the business idea can be used to explain very clearly why even commercial strategies must take social responsibility issues into account. Most business ideas have strong implications not only for what a business will produce, but for the way it will organize itself to do business—its very identity as an organization. A company that does not have, or loses, congruence between its business idea, its strategy, and its social role (its integrity, in the broad sense) is much more likely to make mistakes and to be called to account for them than will a company that has these concepts aligned. In the following cases, we keep this assumption in mind as we explore the recent experiences of several companies.

Royal Dutch/Shell - oil spill, Nigeria

So dramatic was Royal Dutch/Shell's encounter with reputation-threatening forces in 1995 that it is hard to imagine a book on this subject that would not discuss the company's experiences. That year the company was accused of initiating actions that would damage the ocean environment (by disposing of the platform Brent Spar in the North Sea) and of complicity in the executions of nine environmental activists in Nigeria (by aligning itself with its joint venture partner, the Nigerian military government).

Brent Spar - environment

In 1995, Shell's operating company in the United Kingdom, Shell UK, had decided to dispose of a North Sea oil storage tank, the

Brent Spar, in the ocean. The structure had come to the end of its useful life, and Shell's research indicated that ocean disposal was the least environmentally hazardous technique. The company's decommissioning plan was approved by all the required United Kingdom and European government agencies.

Before the plan could be put into effect, however, the international environmental group Greenpeace decided to use Brent Spar to set an example—to prevent ocean disposal from becoming the accepted future means of decommissioning such structures. In a surprise move, the organization landed a group of activists on the Brent Spar and vowed that it would not leave until it had a commitment from Shell that other means of disposal for the facility would be found. After days of intense press coverage, including shots of a water cannon being used to try to dislodge the protesters, the company finally reversed itself and agreed to explore other strategies. The Brent Spar was towed to Norway, where more than two years later a new land-based disposal plan was announced.

Nigeria

Shell's other 1995 crisis was the trial and hanging of Ken Saro-Wiwa, a well-known writer and opponent of the Nigerian military regime, and eight associates. The victims, members of the Ogoni tribe, were accused by the government of conspiring to murder several people who were killed in political clashes in Ogoniland the year before. The clashes themselves were largely the result of battles between Nigerian minority groups and the government, between the groups themselves, and between the groups and Shell over alleged environmental despoliation of their region, the River State, and over the distribution of government oil revenues—local activists felt that more of the government's share of oil generated by Shell in Ogoniland should have been returned to local people for community development.

Saro-Wiwa and his associates were convicted of murder in a military trial that every independent observer considered unfair. Despite worldwide appeals, including from heads of state such as John Major and Nelson Mandela, the Abacha regime hanged the nine activists in November 1995. Protests against Shell broke out around the world; human rights activists accused the company of supporting the well-documented abusive practices of the Nigerian security forces and failing to use its leverage with the government to overturn the death sentences.

On a superficial level, it is possible to say that these events had no short-term effect on the company—at the end of the year, its stock price and profits were at record highs. On a deeper level, the experience had a profound effect. A few markets saw violent protests, attacks on Shell retail outlets, and consumer boycotts. There was widespread comment from the press and public to the effect that Shell's behavior exemplified the stereotype of the irresponsible, indeed evil, multinational. Internally, employees used to being respected for their professionalism and responsibility wrestled with the shock of finding themselves blamed for the tragedies—even their children were being harassed at school.

These events, and the strength of public reaction, seemed to take Shell management by surprise. The company's planning process was one that many companies admired and had wished to emulate—but to outsiders, it did not appear to have helped Shell anticipate what happened to it in Nigeria and the North Sea. So management was doubly hit—by the protests themselves and by its own internal failure to anticipate or prevent the crises. As a Shell executive later told us, the company suddenly realized "how out of tune we were with the world around us."

Most companies under attack go immediately into defensive mode and stay there. Although defense was part of the Shell response, it was, to the company's credit, not all of it. One conclusion that company officials drew from the twin disasters was that they had to revisit their basic planning assumptions in light of public attitudes about the environment and human rights. Another was that they had not been letting enough fresh air into the organization, that they needed a more open dialogue with other stakeholders in their environment—particularly the environmental and human rights NGOs whose protests had been the strongest. A cautious program of outreach to those groups was initiated in an attempt to build dialogue and prevent, if possible, similar conflicts in the future. In particular, Shell decided to make its operations in the Camisea region of Peru a model for a new way of working—to bring in appropriate NGOs at the beginning of the planning process, to allow them access in order to verify the steps Shell was taking, and where necessary, to change the attitudes of group operating companies to social issues.

In 1998, Shell issued its first social responsibility report, entitled *Profits and Principles—Does There Have to Be a Choice?* The publication represented an astonishing reversal to many observers, since at the company's 1997 annual shareholder meeting, retiring chairman John Jennings had stated that the board could not accept activist demands for such a report. The turnaround, coupled with similar moves by mining group Rio Tinto, prompted *Guardian* newspaper columnist Alex Brummer to comment, "Britain's most despised transnational corporations suddenly are leading the world in social accountability." Although many NGO observers interpreted the report as essentially a public relations gesture, others welcomed it as an important first step toward transparency. The report's impact on employees was also strong. It clearly committed the company to a program of standards development, new management systems, independent monitoring practices, and new relationships with stakeholders—a program of which many employees stated they could feel proud.

On the other hand, despite the report's statement that "Shell companies will no longer form joint ventures where partners decline to adopt Business Principles compatible with ours," Shell remains in Nigeria (though not in Ogoniland), and its oil revenues continue to provide a major source of financial support for a regime regarded by most of world opinion as illegitimate and brutally repressive. Although the 1998 death of military leader. Sani Abacha may have opened the door at last toward a more democratic future for Nigeria, it is still true, the Shell report candidly stated, that "One of our dilemmas is how to deal with existing joint venture partners where partners currently reject our Business Principles, or fail to implement them."

The Shell case offers insights both in terms of the historical cycles outlined in the previous chapter and in terms of the significance of the business idea. In both respects, it is important to look at Brent Spar and the Nigerian hangings separately—their superficial similarities (immoral multinational flouts world public opinion) mask very deep differences.

What led Shell into crisis over the Brent Spar was, more than anything else, a too-narrow interpretation of the lessons of history— the general's perpetual danger of fighting yesterday's battle. The model of visibility and concentration leading to reform and constraint had been internalized by Shell, but in terms of traditional control mechanisms (government regulations, for example), which is why the company's technical consultations over disposal techniques focused on the United Kingdom and European governments. Its scanning systems did not include taking Greenpeace and similar organizations seriously as constraining forces. Greenpeace's own credibility was also somewhat compromised by the incident, in that it miscalculated the amount of waste oil left in the tank. Even though Greenpeace acknowledged the mistake as soon as it was discovered, some commentators seized the opportunity to accuse the organization of distorting its science to fit its politics. Nevertheless, Greenpeace's bottom-line assertion (that ocean dumping was not a desirable model for oil rig decommissioning) seemed clearly more in line with public opinion than the United Kingdom government's policy in favor of ocean disposal.

Once this realization was accepted, Shell's policy reversal and subsequent rethink of the disposal issue could be handled in a manner familiar to the company's culture: as a technical problem. The short-term solution was to redefine the problem more broadly, more in keeping with the parameters established by the environmental NGOs; the long-term solution, or beginning of a solution, was to open up discussions with those NGOs and try to find ways to incorporate the organizations into Shell's planning process.

Shell's Nigeria problem shared certain characteristics with the Brent Spar case—especially the "fighting yesterday's battle" part. Yesterday's battle, in Shell's view, was the one we mentioned in Chapter 2, in the boxed section titled "The Imperial Corporation." The lesson Shell learned from that period was that the public did not want multinational companies bossing developing country governments around. In this context, indeed, the company developed its first Statement of General Business Principles. Those principles established a commitment to noninterference by the company in host country political matters, and this commitment became strongly internalized—so strongly that it served as a basis for the company's decision to remain in South Africa throughout the years of antiapartheid sanctions. (The dilemmas inherent in noninterference as a principle were thrown into sharp focus in South Africa nonetheless, especially in terms of Shell's decisions to violate the apartheid laws on behalf of its own employees and eventually to take public positions urging government negotiations with the African National Congress [ANC].) So to a certain extent, Shell's failure to move beyond government consultations in the Brent Spar case had its counterpart in a failure to recognize that the company had marched onto new terrain in Nigeria (or more precisely, that the Nigerian military government had marched onto new terrain).

Nonetheless, the situation faced by Shell in Nigeria was different, and in ways that made the crisis much harder to resolve. It was different because the Brent Spar case, while more dramatic as a controversy, ultimately did not involve a challenge to Shell's basic business idea—adapting to environmental concerns about its business was a process that the company had already begun, if not as quickly or as profoundly as environmentalists might wish. The main problem in Nigeria was not even Shell's commitment to the principle of noninterference, although that principle was a contributing factor and certainly was the factor that was publicly invoked most often. The problem lay with the part of Shell's business idea that formed the company's identity as a *trustworthy partner* to host countries and their governments. From the company's earliest origins, Shell had won competitive advantage over other oil companies by keeping its commitments and delivering what it promised to its partners—a piece of self-image that it valued, for some projects in some markets, even more highly than profit or rate of return. This part of the Shell business idea explains some otherwise illogical behavior—why, for example, it could choose not to do business with the Myanmar junta and yet continue to do business with Sani Abacha. Choosing not to make a commitment in the first place was an easier decision for the company than choosing to break a commitment that Shell had first made in the 1920s, years before Nigerian independence.

The lesson here is that it is much harder for a company to change, or accept the need for change, when an aspect of its core identity is at stake. In Kees van der Heijden's words, the company literally feels as if it is being "asked to commit suicide." As a result, the conclusion to this particular case is a long way from being written. In spring 1997, Shell approved a new version of its Statement of General Business Principles (SGBP)—one that included, for the first time, the term *human rights*. For many human rights NGOs, this statement represented a public relations–level response to the ongoing Nigeria tragedy that fell far short of what was required. From the perspective of this analysis, however, the new statement was a good deal more than just public relations. The Shell SGBP, by long practice, is attached to each joint venture agreement that the company enters into, making the statement by extension part of the company's commitment, including in situations in which the partner is a government or a state-owned enterprise. From the company's perspective, therefore, the inclusion of the term *human rights* in the SGBP meant consciously marching into its own very new territory, territory whose topography is uncertain.

A commitment to supporting human rights, in whatever form the company may define them, that becomes an equal or higher part of Shell's identity than its present values are could mean great changes indeed in the way the company operates. Shell's contracts with indigenous NGOs to provide independent monitoring of its operations in Camisea, Peru, and its newly promulgated Rules of Engagement for security forces may be early indicators of such changes. The shape of the company's operations in China, and whether it can resolve a positive role for itself as the ongoing Nigerian tragedy moves toward reform, will bear watching for similar indicators.

According to a Shell executive involved in drafting the Shell Report, the lessons that the company learned from its experiences in 1995 were profound ones. Here is a brief summary of the salient points:

- "There are no local issues."
  This point reflects the fact that every company decision has the potential to unexpectedly become national or international.
- "Even if you think you're doing the right thing, you may not be."
  This point refers to the company's failure to test its own assumptions with different constituencies.
- "We needed a wake-up call—we've come out stronger than we were before, because now we have set in motion processes we lacked."
- "We should have been thinking about our relationship with society in general in order to see this coming."
- "Bridges must be built with stakeholders at the earliest possible stage, before you are caught between a rock and a hard place."

Interestingly, Greenpeace has recently published a book that details its own learnings from the Brent Spar experience. As summarized in the newsletter *Greenpeace Business,* those lessons were as follows:

- The campaign exposed deep flaws in the relationship between public policy, science, government, and the balancing of public and commercial interests.

  According to Greenpeace, the United Kingdom government contributed at least as much to prolonging the Brent Spar debacle as Shell did and, in fact, was angry at Shell for its reversal. The conflict between the government's twin roles as protector of the environment and as partner to the oil industry was obvious.
- The real impact on industry was psychological and political. Greenpeace's victory forced businesses to reevaluate assumptions about decision making and about relationships with customers and other outsiders, such as environmental groups. (This effect did not just apply to environmental issues. One interviewee for this book described the Texaco diversity case as "Texaco's Brent Spar.")
- The take-home lessons for industry were about values and the public demand for the practices of corporations to reflect public concerns. The real significance of the Spar is as much about corporate responsibility as about oil, or steel, or the ocean.
- Just because actions are legal doesn't mean they are legitimate.
- Fear of controversy now counts.
- [The Brent Spar] was the event that forced the industry most responsible for the world's greatest single environmental problem to begin rethinking its future.

We discuss these lessons more fully in Chapter 10. Whatever else Shell learned from its 1995 disasters, however, one lesson is obvious: the world will, in fact, be watching as the huge company tries to change.

Unocal Mynamar

It is no coincidence that three oil company cases (Shell, Unocal, and Texaco) are included in this book. Over the past century, resource companies have been among those companies most frequently accused of antisocial behavior—not only because of historically poor working and environmental conditions in industries like mining, but also because such companies cannot easily pick and choose where they will operate. They must go where the resource—oil, coal, diamonds, natural gas, water—is to be found, not where the most salubrious partners or markets are. Also, resource companies' projects involve long-term commitments to a location—often 20 or 30 years—during which time a succession of host country governments, of greater or lesser legitimacy, may come and go. In short, companies in the resource sector are much more likely to be seen by the public to have, literally and figuratively, dirty hands.

The other reason we have included both the Shell and Unocal examples in this book is that the two companies' strategic responses to the challenges they face in the area of social responsibility have thus far been different and illustrate the difficulties involved in trying to solve the problem of how—or if—companies should deal with pariah governments. To begin with, the two companies operate on different scales. Shell's annual turnover worldwide is approximately $150 billion from operations in 120 countries. Unocal's turnover is just over $6 billion from operations in more than 20 countries. Unocal's origins are American rather than European—the company is headquartered in California, where it nevertheless announced in 1996 that it planned to spin off all its consumer and retail operations to its 76 Products subsidiary. Although the immediate objective of this divestiture was to free up resources for overseas investment at a higher rate of return than the downstream operations had been earning, it also had the side effect of removing itself from boycott threats arising from its operations in Myanmar (formerly Burma).

It is Unocal's Myanmar operations that most recently have attracted criticism of the company. Like Nigeria, Myanmar is ruled by a military junta that has, as of this writing, refused to recognize election victories by opposition, prodemocracy parties. Since 1990, the State Law and Order Restoration Council (recently renamed the State Peace and Development Council) has held the leader of the National League for Democracy (NLD), Nobel Peace Prize winner Aung San Suu Kyi, under extended house arrest and has imposed increasingly repressive policies against its critics.

Unocal's history in Myanmar illustrates the long project time-scale typical of resource companies. The company first became involved in Burma before the Ne Win era and was forced to leave (along with other foreign firms) by Ne Win's nationalist government. In 1987–1988, Unocal learned that the new government was considering opening its doors again and decided to return to the country for a jump start on a new and undeveloped energy resources. When the military takeover occurred, the company continued its exploration program, partially out of uncertainty over how long the new regime might last. In the words of Unocal president John Imle, "we were not happy about a military government but at that time we were optimistic that things would come right in the end." Imle offered two key facets of the company's criteria for making such choices: the level of corruption involved and the opinion of local managers about whether the overall situation in the country is improving or deteriorating.

Imle's criteria meant that some countries were not considered viable for investment by Unocal, whereas Myanmar was still considered an acceptable investment despite public criticism of the regime and, by extension, of the company. Nevertheless, by 1991–1992 Unocal was considering disinvestment because of an unsuccessful onshore exploration effort. Then French corporation Total won the contract for the Yamada project, a $1.2 billion, 254-mile natural gas pipeline between Thailand and Myanmar and invited Unocal to participate as an investor.

Since its commitment to the Yamada project, Unocal has maintained an aggressive posture in support of its decision to remain in Myanmar. Its public statements have reflected several assumptions that might summarize the classic proengagement (as opposed to prodisinvestment) position:

1. The company's involvement is politically neutral, supporting neither the government nor the opposition. In the words of Unocal's own statement of principles, it is "inappropriate for Unocal to participate in or to support, financially or otherwise, public or private alliances with foreign political parties, opposition movements or other political organisations engaged in the domestic political affairs of a foreign country." In support of this position, the company claims that because of the very long term nature of

energy infrastructure projects, such a project in the end will benefit the people of the country, not any particular government in power at the time the project is undertaken.

2. Engagement "by its nature has to be a positive thing," e.g., the company should refrain from criticizing host government policies except as they directly affect its operations.

3. Where its own operations are involved, the company has achieved specific improvements—on behalf of its Burmese employees or immediate communities. The company cites, for example, the building of schools and health centers, public sanitation projects, and other community development facilities as well as actions to discourage the use of forced labor on non-project-related public works.

4. The company is convinced, therefore, that its involvement in Myanmar "has a net positive impact on the people of that country."

5. Criticism of the Myanmar regime, especially in the form of unilateral sanctions such as those imposed by the United States, is counterproductive and tends to isolate the United States, even from its allies. "The best diplomacy is conducted quietly, not in the headlines."

Unocal remains committed to doing business in Myanmar despite the withdrawal of many other European and American companies in the face of intense criticism from humanitarian and human rights organizations, particularly the Interfaith Center on Corporate Responsibility (ICCR). Because the use of forced labor and conscription on public projects has been well-documented in Myanmar, these organizations have accused Unocal of relying on the Myanmar army to clear indigenous people from the pipeline path and force them under threat to provide support for the pipeline.

Unocal denies that the Myanmar military has had any involvement in the pipeline preparations. The company's March 1997 report on the project asserts that workers are paid under formal contracts and receive wages about 30 percent higher than local averages, adequate to support a family of five. The company also justifies its ties to national security forces because of the threat to its workers by the long-running Karen insurgency (in 1995, 5 civilian workers were killed and 11 others injured). Because the Myanmar government is one of very few in the world that does not allow any independent monitoring organizations to enter the country, human rights organizations say there is no credible verification of Unocal's claims that their operations are an exception to the situations that exist elsewhere in Myanmar; the company claims that there is no credible evidence for linking human rights violations with the pipeline project. According to the U.S. State Department, "the preponderance of the evidence indicates that the pipeline project has paid its workers at least a market wage."

Since passage of sanctions legislation in the United States, large consumer product companies such as Apple, Motorola, and Pepsi (among other U.S. companies) have pulled out of Myanmar, as have several multinationals headquartered in Europe. Unlike these companies, Unocal has not had to fear consumer boycotts (because it has divested its consumer operations in California). The company claims to be under little pressure from shareholders or employees to change its stance, although it acknowledges that some of the religious organizations opposing Unocal's presence in the country are also shareholders and participate in the company's annual shareholder meetings.

In addition to the public criticism generated by its Myanmar activities, Unocal has recently been the target of criticism over its potential role in Afghanistan. The company had proposed to build a gas and oil pipeline from Turkmenistan to Pakistan through Afghanistan, despite harsh criticism from UN agencies and NGOs about the current Taliban governing faction's human rights policies, especially toward women (Taliban policies include prohibitions against employment, appearing in public, or receiving education). The reasons that the company has not gone forward to date with this project are instructive, given the Myanmar precedents: In John Imle's words, the situation "went the wrong way" in Afghanistan, with the Taliban showing no signs of moderating their behavior and the civil war getting worse. In short, the "things that had to happen to be an investable country just didn't happen." In an illustration of the power of one experience to color others, however, Unocal was severely criticized by women's and human rights groups for even making contact with the Taliban as well as other political actors in the country. The NGOs' objections were strengthened by those groups' negative experience with the company over Myanmar.

The question of investment/disinvestment in countries with repressive regimes is one of the most contentious of all questions of social responsibility. One of us tends toward the engagement model, arguing that disinvestment is mostly a public relations gesture and that what counts is a company's commitment to making change happen from within. The other of us tends toward a belief that most companies' commitment to bringing about "change from within" is also a public relations gesture and that executives who do not take the opportunities to stand up for their principles in difficult circumstances forfeit the right to use the engagement argument. We do agree that companies choosing to operate in such conditions must acknowledge that they have taken on enormous responsibility and risk and should expect to be held accountable by the public for what happens on the ground while they are engaged in their business activity. We explore this conflict in more detail in Chapter 5.

How can we apply the concept of the business idea in Unocal's case to learn more about the company's actions over the past decade than we can learn from the company's public statements? A clue can be found in the presentation by the president of Unocal's Asian subsidiary when announcing the Afghanistan pipeline proposal: The presentation stressed Unocal's expertise in working in high-conflict areas, such as Myanmar and areas of Latin America. Far from seeking to avoid such situations, then, the Unocal strategy seems to be to turn their experiences—and willingness to face serious political/ethical challenges investing in controversial countries—into a competitive advantage.

An even more basic aspect of Unocal's decision making helps us understand not only Unocal's but many companies' behavior when faced with these challenges. Most successful business managers are driven to make money, not because they are greedy in the Gordon Gecko sense (as NGOs often assume), but because they want to accomplish things, which is a key distinction that NGOs and other critics need to understand. Media attention is routinely drawn to those few business stars who become millionaires or billionaires, but the vast majority of men (and the few women) who make the sorts of decisions we are analyzing will never become wealthy from their work. They decide to drive on at all costs to complete a project not because they will get a huge salary increase out of it or a big, year end bonus but because it represents tangible accomplishment to them, a monument to their skill and drive. Companies may decide to build a bridge, a canal, or a railroad despite huge costs in money and lives not because they will grow rich (indeed, many go broke) but because they need to complete the task, they need to prove themselves "reliable partners." They may also genuinely believe that the project will improve the lives and economic situations of people in whose countries or regions they are operating. Public criticism therefore leaves them confused and angry. Their task has become the most important value in their lives, and outsiders are telling them, in effect, that they have been wrong, that they have chosen the wrong values.

We return to this issue again in Chapter 6, when we discuss the very different, and in some ways more difficult, task of reperceiving. It is crucial to understanding why companies find defining their responsibilities so hard to do, especially if they firmly believe that (in John Imle's words) "economic progress, fueled by foreign investment, provides the foundation for more democratic and open societies" where international institutions such as the World Bank have indicated a willingness to work with those governments.

At the time of this writing, Unocal's arguments are being weighed against allegations, in U.S. federal courts, against Unocal and Total. One allegation is in the form of a class action on behalf of Burmese people who have been killed, tortured, raped, forcibly relocated, and subjected to forced labor by the Burmese military. Another complaint was brought by the National Coalition Government of Burma (those officials who were democratically elected) and by the Federation of Trade Unions of Burma. It seeks damages from Unocal on the grounds that as a result of the natural gas joint venture, thousands of citizens of Burma represented by the plaintiffs have been subjected to serious human rights abuses in violation of international law and of California tort law. The complaint says that joint venture partner Unocal is vicariously liable for all the human rights violations and money laundering actions taken by the Burmese military in connection with the joint venture.

In a statement filed for a U.S. Department of Labor report to Congress, Unocal responded to the suits by stating that there was no finding in the litigation that Unocal had committed or was responsible for any human rights violations or that it had violated any law. The court did deny a request for a preliminary injunction against the company, taking a relatively narrow view that none of the specific plaintiffs had been forced to work on the pipeline.

A broader legal action was taken against Unocal in September 1998, when a coalition of NGOs filed a petition with the California Attorney General's office to revoke Unocal's corporate charter. According to the petitioners, "the root of the problem is corporate power over sovereign, democratic people." The state, according to the complaint, has the right to revoke the company's power to do business because of Unocal's conduct with respect to environmental practices, workers' rights, and human rights. This legal action is a broader criticism of the company's decisions and a broader assertion about corporate accountability to public opinion than are the earlier lawsuits. This petition directly raises questions such as from where does a company's social "license to operate" derive, and what mechanisms should determine when that broad "license" should be revoked.

Organizations who conduct these campaigns against corporations or file lawsuits are sometimes accused of inconsistency. Why attack Unocal for its activities in Myanmar and not, for example, Exxon for its activities in Saudi Arabia—also a country with a very bad human rights record? Why (until recently) did campaigners attack Shell, and not Mobil or Chevron, for its activities in Nigeria? The answer lies in opportunity, not logic—campaigners choose battles they feel are representative of larger issues *and* contain elements that strengthen their position. As one campaigner sensibly stated, "We have to start somewhere" to make the necessary points. In that sense, companies chosen as targets may feel they are simply unlucky. This attitude is an unhelpful lesson to derive from this analysis, however. The company that responds along these lines is asking, "Why attack us for what we are doing, when x and y are also doing it?" Campaigners are asking entirely different questions: "Why *not* attack you, since what you are doing is wrong whether or not others are doing it too?" or "We are attacking you as a way of demonstrating public opposition to your partner's violations of international law, for which we hold you equally responsible." Companies need to confront and argue out the content of campaigners' criticism, not their choice of strategy or target.

The political and legal context of the Unocal case affects campaigners' strategies differently from the strategies toward Shell in one important respect: Unocal, as a United States–based company, is potentially vulnerable to (although so far unaffected by) unilateral sanctions legislation that has either passed or been introduced at federal, state, and local levels. As of this writing, equivalent sanctions have not been levied against Nigeria by either of Shell's home countries (the United Kingdom or the Netherlands) or by the Commonwealth. Therefore, much of Unocal's energy has gone into trying to make a political case against the U.S. government's use of economic sanctions rather than into dealing directly with the question of its ties to a repressive regime, as Shell has had to do.

The issue of sanctions is worth some extra discussion here, given the directness with which Unocal has challenged the concept, especially the unilateral sanctions often invoked by the United States. From one point of view, sanctions represent a holdover from the days when national governments could actually control the behavior of "their" companies; the increasing ineffectiveness of sanctions today only underscores the relative decline of that control. Part of that ineffectiveness, unfortunately, is in the apparent political hypocrisy of the sanctions process—it is a step seldom taken against powerful nations or nations whose products are vital to a worldwide industry (i.e., Nigeria, Saudi Arabia). From that perspective, opposition to sanctions can appear to be a relatively principled position on behalf of nations too politically weak to defend themselves (Cuba, Myanmar, Iraq). Opposition to unilateral sanctions, in particular, is not confined to corporations; Japan and several European countries plan to challenge the United States position on the issues before the World Trade Organization. Interestingly, the U.S. government itself (at least at the federal level) appears recently to be questioning the effectiveness of unilateral sanctions, given criticism of its practices in the cases of Cuba, Libya, and Vietnam. Questions about the effectiveness of multilateral, broad-based sanctions, such as those in place against South Africa during the apartheid era, are another matter and are explored in Chapter 6.

Although it may be hard to find evidence that sanctions themselves bring about reform in the target countries, it is also hard to find evidence (at least in the short and medium term) that foreign investment itself, in violation of sanctions, brings about reform. Whether it does or not seems to lie not in any benefit intrinsic to investment but in the host country government's ability to manage the investment wisely. Repression in Nigeria and Myanmar, according to most independent observers, has significantly worsened in the past few years, and those governments' greed has largely prevented what foreign investment they do have from lifting anyone out of poverty but themselves and their immediate supporters. (When Nigerian dictator Sani Abacha's son was killed in a helicopter accident, for example, it was reported that he had many millions of dollars in his bank account, and according to many British news reports, when Mrs. Abacha left the country after her husband's death, she was found to be carrying several suitcases full of cash.) We discuss the issue of corruption in greater detail in Chapter 6.

The Unocal case, in short, summarizes the traditional argument for engagement over disinvestment. Given the growing strength of public opinion against regimes such as the one in Myanmar, however, companies who choose to practice engagement are likely to continue with their uphill struggle to prove that their presence is, indeed, contributing to improvements on the ground. Such companies face the additional problem that, even if they are indeed establishing community programs, paying workers well, and otherwise behaving as good corporate citizens, they are linked in the public mind with the bad behavior of their host governments. Particularly in the case of those few countries that are genuine pariah states (like Myanmar or apartheid-era South Africa), the association is simply too strong to overcome unless a company is willing to publicly challenge host government policies, as Shell was able to do in South Africa.

Nestlé infant formula

The Nestlé example takes us from sanctions as a tool of public opinion to boycotts—the modern version of the nineteenth-century Irish invention. According to a CNN *Financial Network* report, the Nestlé boycott was probably the most global boycott. It lasted 10 years before being called off in 1984, but then was reinstated in 1988.

The issue that caused Nestlé so much trouble was a product that accounts for approximately one percent of its international sales: infant formula. First health officials and then consumer groups became concerned at the effects in developing countries of Nestlé's marketing campaigns for its breast milk substitutes. The position these advocates took was that Nestlé, by aggressively promoting formula, was discouraging the practice of breastfeeding among poor women—a problem both because breast milk is well-established to be the healthiest food for newborns and because substitutes require the addition of water, which exposes children to risks of infection and malnutrition through the generally poor quality of water in the target countries.

After seven years of pressure by newly formed advocacy groups such as the Infant Feeding Action Coalition (INFACT), the International Baby Food Action Network (IBFAN), and others, Nestlé and other firms in the market agreed to a World Health Organization (WHO) code on advertising and promotion of milk substitutes. The code imposed labeling requirements, prohibited distribution of free samples for marketing purposes, and set up other guidelines to which the companies agreed. As a result, the boycott was called off in 1984.

In 1988, consumer groups reinstated the boycott, accusing the signatory companies, and Nestlé in particular, of violating the code to which they had agreed, largely in terms of failing to meet labeling requirements and returning to the large-scale distribution of free samples. In 1994, IBFAN published a report called *Breaking the Rules 1994,* which summarized many of the accusations, and British television picked up the theme in a documentary shown in 1995. In 1997, the nutrition section of UNICEF's annual report accused the companies of failing to comply with the code, stating that improved breastfeeding practices could save the lives of 1.5 million children annually. Nestlé's management has argued in response that it has not committed most of the violations it has been accused of and that where the violations were found to exist, the company had corrected them.

Boycotts like the one against Nestlé usually have two goals: to damage company financial performance and to cause long-term damage to the company's image. It is almost impossible to prove that boycotts accomplish the former, except with enormous effort in a small-scale context (i.e., the black boycott of segregated buses in Montgomery, Alabama). At the national or international level, even boycotts called by large and credible organizations (the NAACP, Southern Baptist Convention, etc.) have trouble demonstrating that their campaigns against companies like Disney have a discernible impact. Boycotts have achieved some success in the long-term image area: A company becomes concerned about being associated with racist values or exploitation of developing country markets or employee morale and decides to take action to prevent this type of tarnishing.

Another aspect of boycotts that often makes them difficult for companies to respond to, or to take seriously, is that their organization (if there is any) can be extremely amorphous. As one researcher stated, there are many more calls for boycotts than there are actual campaigns. The major accomplishment of the Nestlé boycott—achievement of the WHO code—came about because specific organizations formed around the boycott and were willing to campaign in a focused, relatively well-funded manner for 10 years. Even with the aid of such factors, calls to launch, end, or reinstate a boycott seldom result in clear consequences. Once some participants get into the habit, they go on boycotting a product for years without even caring if the official boycott is still on; the vast majority of consumers could probably not name a single boycott currently listed on the Boycott Board Web site.

The nature of the Internet has made the notion of a boycott even harder to pin down. There are literally hundreds of Web sites at which consumers can find information on boycotts, some apparently launched by one angry person. The larger sites disclaim any responsibility for the veracity of claims, or even for whether a listed boycott actually exists, thus increasing the likelihood that only the already committed will respond to the call.

The legitimacy of the Nestlé boycott was enormously aided, of course, by the involvement of health professionals and, in the end, of United Nations–related agencies in spreading information about the company's practices. Because most such efforts do not have these institutional supports, corporations generally respond to consumer boycott initiatives less because of the threat of immediate, short-term financial damage than because of the possibility of long-term weakening of the brand.

Texaco – Racism

On November 4, 1996, the racial fault line running through American society opened wide, and Texaco was standing over it. Texaco, our third oil company example, was already dealing with a race discrimination suit filed by six black employees in 1994, a suit that in itself was the result of a major personal turning point for the main plaintiff, Bari-Ellen Roberts. As she notes in her book, *Roberts v. Texaco,* the action would probably not have been taken if not for one crucial meeting between herself, an African-American colleague, and the head of Texaco's human resource department. In this meeting, she alleged, the executive reacted angrily to several prodiversity initiatives that she and her colleague had prepared in response to a request from company management. This response was the proverbial last straw for the two and helped set in motion the chain of events that led to one of the most intense examinations of racism in the workplace ever seen in the United States.

Management had not considered the suit a particularly serious threat until that day in November when the plaintiffs' lawyers released to the *New York Times* a tape of Texaco executives allegedly making racist comments and conspiring to conceal company documents. A publicity firestorm broke over the company, with television reporters trying to capture videotape of the corporate headquarters, with calls for boycotts being issued, and with front-page battles being waged over what words were, or were not, spoken on the tape.

In retrospect, Texaco management saw two crucial decisions as turning points in the controversy during those early days of the crisis. First, new Texaco CEO Peter Bijur chose not to join the literal war of words over the tapes themselves. As one executive stated, whether a specific racial epithet was uttered was beside the point; the "ugly laughter" they heard, once the tapes were made available to them, was enough to prove that they had a problem to solve. In making this decision management chose not to complain that Texaco was being held to a standard no other U.S. company could meet, but instead chose to try to "create a benefit out of it" and make achieving diversity a positive competitive advantage. As CEO Bijur described it, the incident became "a clarion call to start something different in the company." Two weeks after the *New York Times* article appeared, the company agreed to a $115 million settlement to its nority employees, a one-time salary increase, and $30 mi¹" programs to improve the racial climate within the orga⸍ company also reached out to the African-Ameri⸍ with CEO Bijur personally seeking out leaders ⸍ rist Leon Higginbotham for advice and counse⸍

When asked about this crisis period, Pete⸍ 45-day period of crafting the Texaco correc⸍

from the second major turning point: the decision to produce a plan that represented a serious long-term commitment instead of a public relations response. "When you're under great pressure, it's tempting to do what people want you to do instead of what's actually good for your company to do," Bijur said. The substantive program, put together by a team of internal employees with some external assistance on benchmarking, looked at similar experiences at Denny's Avis, Ford, and Coca-Cola. The plan, when outlined to the civil rights community at the company's Washington offices, was well received, and the company moved immediately to implementation.

The rapid responses and direct action of Texaco's CEO were widely credited with heading off any more long-term negative impact of the dramatic revelations. Bijur's behavior was perceived by employees as open and not arrogant. It also contrasted strongly with the response of other companies to similar crises—Exxon's widely criticized response to the Exxon Valdez oil spill, for example. (As a *Fortune* magazine article stated in 1990, "(Exxon) management has repeatedly underestimated public reaction to the spills and contrives to talk as though the public has nothing at stake. CEO Rawl says he didn't go to Alaska at once because the clean-up was in capable hands and he had 'many other things to do.' "

Although Texaco management might have mishandled its minority workforce's earlier complaints, its response to the crisis itself was clearly not like the Exxon model. In fact, the point of making the settlement was to get on immediately with solving the problem rather than to argue about the legitimacy of the accusations. Since the settlement, Texaco has followed through with its planned internal programs of employee training and has also undertaken specific steps to increase diversity at board and staff level. Employees, by and large, feel that they were able to create important learnings and benefits out of a situation that initially threatened to overwhelm the company; in the fall of 1997, 85 percent of Texaco's workforce stated in response to a questionnaire that they recognized the importance of diversity to their business.

Like Shell, Texaco has released public reports on its progress toward diversity goals. The company's Equality and Fairness Task ce, which was the outside monitoring system established as part xaco's settlement, reported to the U.S. district court in early

1998 that during 1997, nearly 40 percent of the 8,904 new hires in Texaco's U.S. operations were racial and ethnic minorities, and fully half were women. Women earned 44 percent of the 599 promotions at Texaco during 1997, and minorities earned 25 percent. Direct expenditures by the company on minority and women-owned businesses rose $159 million over the previous year, to 7.1 percent of total discretionary expenditures. (Interestingly, this outside monitoring committee was an aspect of the settlement to which CEO Bijur first objected, but later came to see as a valuable source of credibility for the company's efforts.)

The committee's report underscores another significant aspect of the Texaco settlement. Although the plaintiffs' case involved racial discrimination, the settlement includes gender as well as racial diversity initiatives (despite the fact that Texaco already had more women in senior positions than did most other oil companies). This attempt to deal with the corporate glass ceiling in a long-term way reflects the increasing importance of women's employment and other gender issues in social responsibility programs.

As a final note, Texaco management shared with us their major learnings from this experience. Those lessons have broad applicability and are summarized here:

- "We learned that we could be doing more with our programs and setting higher goals and objectives both in hiring and retention and in business partnering activities."

  Despite some progress in minority representation in Texaco between 1988 and 1996, management found after the crisis that they could not only put forward a more aggressive plan but achieve it as well.

- "Texaco is a microcosm of society."

  As part of the United States of America, the Texaco organization was bound to have among its employees some who would have racist views and would act on them if allowed. The management learned that although they might not be able to change attitudes, they could expect to influence behavior by establishing a new policy of "zero tolerance for intolerance."

- "What happened at Texaco can happen at any company—and having the right policies and directives in place is simply not enough."

This lesson addresses the degree of management insistence on change and the company's incentive structure. Texaco's compensation system now includes performance measurements, which affect managers' bonuses, that are related to their achievement of diversity goals.

- Texaco learned "the need for focus and personal leadership during a crisis."

The CEO's responsibility is to lead the company during a crisis, not to get sidetracked by peripheral issues and delegate the running of the business to others. This theme runs through every case we studied.

Union Carbide - Bophol

The Union Carbide case offers proof that the Internet has provided, in addition to boycott updates, a new channel for both companies and campaigners to make their cases to the public. After 13 years, concerned citizens can still visit Union Carbide's Bhopal Web site and read updates of the continuing medical problems, legal battles, and hospital construction plans connected to the lethal gas leak—illustrating the ongoing impact of the world's worst industrial accident, which killed 3,800 people and injured up to half a million.

Two major technical investigations, one conducted by the Indian government and one sponsored by Union Carbide Corporation USA (UCC) with scientists and engineers from UCC, from Union Carbide India Limited (UCIL), and from Arthur D. Little Consulting, ended in disagreement on the cause of the leak. The Indian government claimed that improper safety procedures during a routine operation caused water to enter a tank of methyl isocyanate (MIC) and react with it to create the cloud of poisonous gas, whereas the UCC/ADL team instead found evidence of sabotage in the form of a large quantity of water being introduced directly into the tank via a hose.

Whatever the proximate cause, the following conditions combined to create the massive disaster that followed:

1. neither the Indian government nor UCIL's management were knowledgeable about the potential dangers of MIC production. . . .

2. many technical malfunctions and human errors compounded the leak ...

3. the immediate population of Bhopal was ignorant of any danger (associated with the plant)...the Labour Minister opposed moving the plant (despite zoning requirements) because the trade union objected ...

4. the local authorities, also ignorant, commanded the population to flee...not knowing that a better strategy would have been to lie on the ground and breathe through a damp cloth....

5. the poor infrastructure of the city contributed to a lack of effectiveness of emergency efforts.

The question of legal and moral accountability for the deaths and injuries immediately became politicized, partly because of the upheavals and violence still taking place in India after Indira Gandhi's assassination a month earlier. The government arrested Warren Anderson, Union Carbide chairman, when he arrived in Bhopal days later (he was quickly released), and subsequently refused for more than a year to allow UCC staff to interview UCIL employees. The Indian government also initially rejected millions of dollars in relief funds from UCC; the Indian Red Cross finally accepted and used most of the money to assist victims.

UCC took pains to distance itself from UCIL, which it had established 50 years earlier and in which it was a 50.9 percent owner. The company insisted that India was the proper site for litigation, not the United States, and U.S. courts agreed. The case dragged on for four years until, in 1989, the Indian Supreme Court directed a settlement of $470 million and nullified criminal charges. After the next Indian election, the new government repudiated the court decision, and it was another four years before the settlement was reaffirmed and settlement funds began to flow.

In the years following, Union Carbide management admitted on their own Web site to having been smug about their earlier safety record and promised to commit money and staff to reducing risk. In 1989, despite UCC's claim of "substantial improvement in reducing the emission and discharge of toxic waste," the Council on Economic Priorities found "no consistent and overriding pattern of progress" on the company's part. The chemical industry response to Bhopal included establishment of community action emergency response programs in the United States and similar initiatives in 22 countries.

In January 1994, the International Medical Commission on Bhopal (IMCB), a team of health experts from 12 countries, visited the city. In their summary statement of December 1996, the IMCB found that 94 percent of the gas-exposed subjects continued to experience health problems and that the compensation courts set up to administer the settlement had "little understanding of health problems related to gas exposure." The team found that both Union Carbide and the Indian government had contributed to the failure of medical care by failing to release information about toxicology and health studies to their mutual distress. Whereas Union Carbide and the Indian government have focused on construction of new hospitals, one of which finally opened in 1998, the IMCB has called instead for creation of outpatient, community-based clinics. A survivor-run clinic opened in 1996.

Bhopal has been compared with the Three Mile Island and Chernobyl nuclear disasters as an example of failure to design and plan for inconceivable events and as a reflection of the technological arrogance to which engineering cultures are susceptible. The Bhopal situation had the added complication of technology translated into a different industrial culture, less protected against error. As Paul Shrivastava has summarized it, "The plant was operated by a company under pressure to make profits and/or cut losses; it was sanctioned by a government under pressure to industrialise, even though the appropriate industrial infrastructure and support systems were missing; and it was located in a city completely unprepared to cope with any major accident." Of the specific cases cited in this book, Bhopal has caused the most death and injury, and yet we have no reason to believe that it could not happen again—a maquiladora factory, a bioengineering facility, or a weapons plant in any number of countries could fit Shrivastava's description.

As Mitroff observed, we as a society have apparently decided to tolerate this threat; indeed, in the developed world, we see an increasing trend toward a response not of increased investment in safety technologies or more intelligent regulation but of exporting the problem. The "clean" processes are done at home; the "dirty" ones are laundered as foreign investment, to the applause of local constituents. (A tiny illustration of this process brings us back, briefly, to the Brent Spar. The son of one of the authors was at a rock concert in Britain when the news was announced from the stage that Shell had capitulated to Greenpeace and that the Brent Spar would be "towed to Norway." The crowd roared, and the boy wondered for an instant whether the reaction expressed more pleasure at dumping the United Kingdom's garbage somewhere else or at the victory over Shell.) This trend to export the problem is a fortuitous convergence of the drives for lower costs and for less particular neighbors. In addition, the parent-subsidiary bond has been stretched past the breaking point in many instances, resulting in situations in which the developing country facility is legally no more than a contractor and therefore even less subject to "best practice" standards.

What is interesting, then, is that public opinion seems less willing to follow the corporate lead and to limit accountability to the foreign contractor or subcontractor. The legal firewalls that companies in developed countries have tried to build between themselves and their overseas manufacturing bases are becoming invisible to a large portion of the public. From a contemporary environmental perspective, the case of Thor Chemicals later in this chapter illustrates a potentially important shift in the legal assumptions that allowed Union Carbide to prevent Bhopal-related litigation from being handled by U.S. courts. In a nonenvironmental context, the Council on Economic Priorities' new sourcing Standard 8000 explicitly assumes that a company is accountable for the employment practices of its contractors and subcontractors. The next case represents a good example of a company caught by surprise by the new paradigm.

Nike

"Nike boss Phil Knight's 1994 salary was $1,500,000. On current wages, a young woman in China churning out his shoes would have to work nine hours a day, six days a week for 15 centuries to match that."

In a nutshell, this statement sums up the issue that brought hundreds of demonstrators out to the 1996 opening of Nike's new store in San Francisco. Organizations such as Christian Aid in the United Kingdom, the National Labor Alliance in the United States, and trade unions in developing countries have spent the past several years examining the global production processes of apparel and sporting goods companies and have found that many of them earn the familiar description of sweatshop.

Training shoes have, for several reasons, become a particular target of the campaigns of these organizations: Ninety-nine percent of world production comes from Asia, generally from the same countries and suppliers; the biggest companies (Reebok, Nike, Adidas, Hi-Tec, and Puma) differentiate their products not by cost or quality but by image and design; and that image is much more visible than the image of most apparel items. Therefore the contrast between the corporate images of these training shoe companies and the reality of working conditions in their contractors' factories is more striking than for other types of apparel.

According to Nike, its products are priced in multiples of 1-2-4. In other words, the company buys a product from a factory for $20; it adds transportation and marketing costs plus profit, and it sells that product to the retailer for $40; the retailer in turn adds similar costs and profits and sells the product to the consumer for $80. Christian Aid's researchers found that the average labor cost of these shoes across the three countries of China, the Philippines, and Thailand was $1.44 and therefore have put forward the argument that the companies can afford to significantly increase workers' wages while scarcely changing the final consumer price at all. (In this model, a worker making $1.44 per pair of shoes could receive a 50 percent increase in pay that would increase the final cost of the shoes by less than $3.)

All the companies listed here have found themselves put on the defensive by the NGOs' campaigns, especially Reebok because of its long association with human rights issues and other progressive corporate policies. According to Christian Aid, Nike initially responded to criticism by taking the following positions:

a. the workers are lucky . . . it's better than having no job.
b. it is not the companies' business . . . you should be asking that question of the United Nations.
c. they are indeed dealing with the problem, giving concrete instances of action taken.

The company's confusion and surprise has some basis in reality. In general, "the subcontractors used by the major sports shoe companies are not among the worst employers in their countries... most workers are paid the minimum wage and receive fringe benefits." For several reasons, however, Nike and its competitors could have seen the criticism coming:

- They have consciously, and at great cost (Nike spent $280 million on advertising in 1994), marketed an image of themselves as leaders, doing better than just good enough at their job.
- The contrast between the income of company spokespeople and the income of company workers is much greater than in other industries (forget Phil Knight; Andre Agassi reportedly received $70 million from Nike to endorse tennis clothing).
- As we noted in the case of Union Carbide, the general public no longer distinguishes between contract employees and "real" employees, holding the company as responsible for one as for the other.
- The sport shoe and apparel companies have demonstrably shopped the developing world, moving contracts out of countries in which wages are rising and into countries in which wages are still lowest.
- Although most people would agree with Nike that any job is better than no job, people are not necessarily willing to tolerate poor wages and working conditions indefinitely. Eating bark is also better than starving, but most of us would not wish either one for our children.

The Nike case, in short, appears to confirm a statement by a garment industry representative in a 1996 *Wall Street Journal* article:

I am not speaking as a do-gooder. I do not now nor have I ever belonged to any organization with the words "People for," "Friends of," or even "Help" in its title. I am a garment industry consultant who has spent 30 years in Asia showing companies how to produce and buy better garments for less money. And I know for a fact that no social adjustments take place in the world of business unless the cost-accountants prove that change is necessary. But I am here to tell you that the tapping noise you hear on your door is your CPA coming to announce that something is indeed happening out there, and that if you want to survive, now would be a good time to develop a social conscience.

In the spring of 1998, as industry gadfly Michael Moore's interview with Phil Knight was reaching American cinemas in *The Big One,* Knight made a dramatic speech to the National Press Club in which he acknowledged not having understood the depth of public concern on the issue of worker exploitation and announced several new policies that the company would begin enforcing. These new policies included launching a new design that avoided use of toluene, a hazardous chemical previously widely used in shoe production; supporting a series of research initiatives and conferences on international manufacturing practices; and initiating a program of independent monitoring of Nike factories. The policies did not address questions of wage levels. Knight acknowledged that the company's plans would not go far enough to satisfy all its critics; significantly, however, he concluded by saying that the program would make workers at Nike "feel better about ourselves."

When a company's reputation is under attack, charges that are false or unproven are more easily taken seriously. After Knight's speech, Nike became involved with a new controversy arising from the World Cup football finals—the allegation (that was false) that the company, along with other major athletic sponsors, put Brazil's star player at risk and contributed to the disastrous showing of his team by pressuring him to play despite serious injury. The incident, whether or not true, and although not directly related to the manufacturing practice scandals, helped nonetheless to support the impression of Nike as a company whose commercial interests had overwhelmed both its humanity and its sportsmanship.

Perhaps the company's public commitment to improved conditions in its subcontractors' factories—and the effectiveness of the advertising campaigns from Nike and other sports shoe manufacturers—will allay public concern about Nike's manufacturing and commercial practices. One California teenager told us that his resolve never to buy Nike products was shaken when he saw a recent commercial that included his favorite soccer stars endorsing the brand. But his friend also told us about a player on their school team who literally cut the Nike swoosh off his sneakers and uniform—the tapping noise at the door of Nike's future?

The broad uproar over the apparel industry's offshore operations, which spread to dozens of firms, even involved the U.S. White House. The federal government helped organize 10 apparel companies along with several concerned NGOs into the Apparel Industry Partnership (AIP). The task for the group is to put enforcement into their existing codes of conduct, which for the government and NGOs, means a program of independent monitors who can make unannounced visits and speak to the contractors' workforce directly. It is not clear at this point how effective the AIP will be. Membership is voluntary, and even existing members have problems both with elements of the code itself (particularly wage issues) and with implementation of the monitoring requirements. Nonetheless, such initiatives as *Standard 8000,* the AIP, and the Apparel, Footwear, and Retailing Working Group of the organization Business and Social Responsibility will increasingly make similar demands on other firms, and noncompliance with developing international standards will become more expensive over time.

A larger question is whether these pressures will force widespread change in the system of international manufacturing that has been so spectacularly successful under globalization. If so, and if the result is positive (from the perspective of the living-wage movement), this change could represent a modern version of the domination–crisis–regulation/control sequence that we outlined in Chapter 2. In the March–April 1998 issue of *Foreign Affairs,* Debora Spar argues that western multinationals, because of their vulnerability to public opinion, will ultimately become exporters of human rights to developing country workforces, raising wages and other national labor standards as the companies spread from country to country. This optimistic view is the opposite of Korten's thesis of manufacturers' "race to the bottom." It also applies mainly to the consumer goods industry because, as we have seen in the oil company cases presented here, not all sectors are equally vulnerable to public opinion.

A. H. Robins

In our introduction, we stated that the companies we would be examining were not companies that had, among other things, made fraudulent product claims—but the case of A. H. Robins and the Dalkon Shield begins to slip into a gray zone. A contraceptive device (important definition, because the word "device" enabled the company to avoid Food and Drug Administration [FDA] approval procedures), the Dalkon Shield was invented in 1968 by a gynecologist and an electrical engineer who initially tested their new product on clients of a family planning clinic operated by Johns Hopkins Medical School in Baltimore. The two attempted, in their design, to overcome two main problems of earlier intrauterine devices (IUDs): their tendency to be ejected from the uterus and their tendency to wick infectious bacteria into the uterus through the cervix. Using test results that were later proved to have been misrepresented, the gynecologist/inventor published an article in the *American Journal of Obstetrics and Gynecology* announcing an annual pregnancy rate much lower than that of previous IUDs and making no mention of any significant adverse effects.

In 1970, the A. H. Robins company, primarily engaged in the pharmaceutical business and with no experience in the contraceptive field, purchased the rights to the Dalkon Shield and began a high-powered marketing campaign. The campaign, addressed not only to gynecologists but also to general practitioners and to women themselves, resulted in more Dalkon Shields being sold by 1971 than all other brands of IUDs combined. Unfortunately, in 1971 a Robins quality control employee also produced the first evidence that wicking of bacteria through the shield could be a problem. This concern was not followed up. By 1972, physicians were beginning to contact Robins with accounts of spontaneous abortions occurring in women wearing the shields, and in 1973 the first two women died—of severe sepsis, or infection. In 1974, after Robins learned that a medical journal article on maternal death and the Dalkon Shield was due to be published, the company finally suspended sales in the United States—but continued foreign sales for another 10 months in at least 40 foreign countries. By early 1975, 15 women in the United States had died and several hundred suits had been filed against Robins.

Robins' strategy, as documented in court records and the press, was initially to blame physicians and later to blame the women— including cross-examining women about their sexual habits. By 1980, almost a thousand new cases were being filed each year, and Robins finally notified physicians that they should consider removing the shields from any women still wearing them. The company still resisted a full-scale product recall. One judge in Minnesota, in his approval of a settlement agreement between Robins and two injured women, pleaded with the company: "If this were a case in equity, I would order your company to make an effort to locate each and every woman who still wears this device and recall your product. But this court does not have the power to do so. I must therefore resort to moral persuasion and a personal appeal to each of you.... Please, in the name of humanity, lift your eyes above the bottom line."

Eight months later, after a company whistle-blower produced copies of documents he had been ordered to shred, Robins did initiate a recall campaign. By that time, 7,700 legal cases had been settled at a cost of $260 million, and another 3,500 were pending, with 10 new cases being filed every day. By the spring of 1985, Robins was facing financial collapse, and in July its stock dropped 50 percent. In August Robins filed for bankruptcy in Richmond, Virginia, its longtime headquarters. The action stopped all proceedings against Robins and began a five-year legal battle that ultimately involved 195,000 plaintiffs and resulted in the sale of Robins to American Home Products (AHP).

At the beginning of the bankruptcy case, attorneys for several of the injured women asked for a dismissal, arguing that the bankruptcy motion had been filed not in good faith but instead to consolidate the cases into a single class action suit before a sympathetic judge and to avoid disclosure of documents that could lead to criminal prosecution of Robins officials. By the end of the bankruptcy action, these suspicions looked to have been well founded. Not only were the Robins family executives protected from criminal prosecution, they benefited handsomely from the sale to AHP ($385 million to the family). In 1990 the plaintiffs finally began receiving limited compensation payments, based on a sliding scale of damage, from a $2.45 billion trust fund. The judge never did allow a single female victim to testify during the bankruptcy proceeding and indeed ejected one from the courtroom when she tried to speak out in anger at the conclusion of the case.

The Robins case echoes the handling, in British courts, of the thalidomide disaster. The British distributor of thalidomide, Distillers Company Biochemicals Ltd. (DCBL), also adopted a highly defensive position and the result was that it also took 15 years (1962–

1977) to reach agreement on compensation for the victims. In both cases, early signs of serious side effects resulted in a redoubling of marketing efforts instead of renewed clinical investigations; in fact, "[Distillers] were prepared to invest psychologically and financially in a prolonged legal and publicity battle." Even the fact that the victims were highly sympathetic figures—severely deformed babies in one case, young women dying, experiencing severe injury, or living with childlessness in the other case—seemed to carry no weight with the companies compared to what they saw as their overriding commercial interests.

A startling recent development, and possible harbinger of change, in the pharmaceutical industry has been the reemergence of thalidomide on the market. As reported in the *New York Times* on January 25, 1998, the discovery that the drug was extremely effective against a variety of immune-deficiency disorders gave the leadership of the Thalidomide Victims' Assocation (TVA) "the moral quandary of the century." Should they cooperate with Celgene, the company that was proposing to make the drug available to AIDS victims, leprosy patients, and other victims of immune system disease? Could they be sure that they would not end up complicit in the harming of more children, whose suffering nobody could possibly understand better? If the TVA did not cooperate, would adulterated forms of the drug, already being illegally imported, end up causing similar disasters? And what about the Celgene executive hired to develop a marketing plan for, of all things, thalidomide? How would he deal with the activists whose lives had been distorted forever by the drug?

The questions facing both the TVA and Celgene had their most immediate antecedents in the battle between "big pharma" (in particular, Burroughs-Wellcome) and AIDS activists. Burroughs-Wellcome first introduced azidothymidine (AZT, a powerful drug used in the treatment of HIV/AIDS), using a traditional approach to introduction and pricing. On the occasion of Burroughs' initial public offering (IPO), ACT-UP, the AIDS organization, poured blood on the floor of the Stock Exchange. The initially violent confrontations between industry and health care activists have, with some difficulty, transmuted into a system of working groups in which industry and community health groups lobby jointly for common causes. Celgene's familiarity with this experience and the year that it spent studying the TVA's activities led it eventually to approach the TVA.

In what both sides described as a "very, very hard meeting" in Toronto, the marketer and the "thalidomider" (the TVA term) began a long process that eventually led to an agreed protocol on the distribution of thalidomide—at least until an analogue without side effects is created.

The eventual decisions made by people on both sides of the current thalidomide quandary are instructive—not only in contrast to the behavior of Robins, DCBL, and Grunenthal (the original German manufacturer of thalidomide) but also in possible signposting of new forms of advocate-industry relationships. The TVA's Canadian CEO, Randy Warren, and Celgene decided to cooperate rather than do battle. Bruce Williams, Celgene marketing manager, made his decision not just because he felt he had no choice but also because he felt that most of what Randy Warren had said in position papers was aligned with the company's thinking on issues like labeling, regulation, and other forms of risk control. Warren in turn made his decision not only because Celgene did agree to most of the association's demands but also because the company committed to continue investing in a research program to develop a safe replacement for thalidomide.

Both Celgene and the TVA were working with a much broader definition of "stakeholder" than organizations often use, and that breadth is what enabled them to reach agreement on a resolution of their mutual moral quandary. For Warren, the result of the TVA's year-long internal consultation was a tribute to "the outstanding pragmatism of our group and its empathy for others." In language reminiscent of those who choose engagement over disinvestment, he stated: "I want to see thalidomide devastated, but I want to be there to see it, not on the outside looking in." Celgene marketing manager, Bruce Williams, has been quoted as saying that he now asks himself, with every decision, what Randy would think about that—a thought process in strong contrast to the thoughts, 17 years ago, of executives of A. H. Robins.

Stepping Over the Line

Now that we have spent a few pages in the gray area, let's conclude with a trip to the black zone to contrast the our earlier examples with more outright corporate criminality.

The Bofors Case

A case that still roils Indian and Swedish politics is the arms deal involving Swedish weapons manufacturer Bofors. The situation began in 1986, when Indian prime minister Rajiv Gandhi and Swedish prime minister Olof Palme concluded what was described as a government-to-government deal for the gunmaker to sell to India $1.3 billion worth of Howitzers. Bofors was having financial problems, and the Swedish government was trying hard to help it win additional international contracts. (The interaction between governmental agendas—jobs and economic development—and corporate ones is a theme we return to in Chapter 7.) India's chief of army staff later complained that political pressure was put on him to select the Swedish equipment rather than the French supplies that the army preferred.

A 1997 *Forbes* magazine article has said that despite the deaths of both prime ministers soon afterward, "the case refuses to die." Some commentators have tried to link the Palme assassination to the Bofors case. The Indian Central Bureau of Investigation has filed bribery charges against several men and women, including the late Prime Minister Gandhi, and it claims to have established that $250 million of the arms sale amount was paid in bribes. In addition to Palme's, several other people connected with the investigation died under mysterious circumstances, and investigative reporters working on the case received threats and offers of cash themselves. In the 1989 elections, Rajiv Gandhi's Congress Party majority was wiped out, in large part because of Bofors and accusations by his political opponents that Gandhi was "a thief."

Although no prosecutions have yet been undertaken on this case, the impact of it is still enormous, even after 10 years. Governments continue to rise and fall in the wake of accusations of complicity in this and related scandals. Efforts are still being made by Indian authorities to extradite from Switzerland the Gandhi family confidant who supposedly served as the go-between for illegal payments. And India's former ambassador to Sweden, B. M. Oza, has recently stated, "the long saga of the still continuing and still unfolding Bofors scandal has been a chapter of national shame and trauma . . . the quality of our public life has gone down . . . what are the reasons? Taking Bofors as a case study [allows us to] examine this phenomenon."

The Bofors case illustrates, among other things, today's difficulties in international prosecutions of even outright corporate criminal behavior. The normal obstacles of international jurisdictional issues, banking secrecy laws, and document recovery are compounded, in the Bofors case, by involvement of government agencies and political interests (a not uncommon situation). Even when those factors are absent, bringing a successful case against an international corporation is something of an expensive rarity. As the next example indicates, however, some aspects of the legal environment may be changing.

Thor Chemicals

Thor Chemicals, a British firm, decided in 1987 (under pressure from the United Kingdom Health and Safety Executive) to move its major mercury plant from Margate to South Africa. In 1989, Greenpeace began to sample rivers around the South African plant, the largest in the world, and discovered mercury levels "3200 times that allowed by regulation in the United States." As the Minamata experience in Japan illustrated, mercury poisoning is devastating in its scope and damaging effects. By 1997, four of Thor's South African workers had died of mercury poisoning, one lay in a coma, and another 24 had suffered crippling neurological damage. When the company's workers discovered the cause of their illnesses, they attempted to sue the company but found that South African legislation prohibited workers from suing their employers.

Eventually criminal charges were filed against plant management, and in 1995 the company was fined approximately $5,500. According to James Cameron, writing in the *Asia-Pacific Journal of Environmental Law,* "The Thor Chemicals case became a symbolic one in post-apartheid South Africa. Nelson Mandela has visited affected workers in hospitals...one of the consequences of mercury poisoning is that it brings on delirium, often followed by coma and death." A grisly measure of South African reaction to the case was the abduction and murder of a British executive of Thor whose dismembered body was found in his BMW, smeared with mercury-contaminated sludge from the plant.

After the unsatisfactory South African legal result, the workers attempted to sue in British courts, and in a precedent-setting decision, the House of Lords agreed that jurisdiction could not fairly remain with the courts of the country of operation. (According to one

of the plaintiff's lawyers, a turning point in the case came when photographs of the comatose and disabled workers were shown to
judges—another indication of the power of communications in
forming public responses, similar to the campaigning that eventually
won a conviction for the Minamata victims). A similar decision on
behalf of a Scottish uranium worker, an employee of RTZ, meant,
according to a dissenting judge, that any multinational could be sued
in England with respect to its activities anywhere in the world if its
parent company is in England.

Another commentator analyzed the outcome: "Legal standards of
corporate responsibility are rising around the world, in some cases
markedly...a company's performance in one jurisdiction with relatively low standards may be judged with reference to the higher legal
standards of another. Thor's experiences, in particular, demonstrate
that it is not acceptable for companies to operate to standards which
fall below those which would be required of them in their home
countries."

If this trend continues, it will represent to companies a new face
of globalization. Companies that do observe the same high safety
standards worldwide would find themselves at less competitive risk
from lowest-common-denominator companies, at least the multinational ones. On the other hand, the trend may simply drive parent
firms out of their original host country jurisdictions. The jury, figuratively (and maybe literally), is still out—but imagine the difference
in the financial outcome of the Bhopal case, for example, if it had
been tried in U.S. courts and the scale of the stakes involved had become clear.

Summary: Phases of a Crisis

As we indicated in the beginning of the book, our main interest is
not to focus on examples of outrageous behavior, as we saw in the
Thor and Bofors cases. Legal systems do exist, however clumsy or
weak, to deal with this behavior, and established organizations like
trade unions have been effective in bringing such cases forward to
public attention. Most important, though, responsible companies
generally have internal warning systems in place to detect criminal
activity on the part of employees, or they have management performance standards that include being alert to safety or environmen-

tal hazards. As a result, in responsible companies, episodes like those that occurred at Thor (or even, perhaps, at A. H. Robins) would likely have been prevented and a full-scale public relations crisis avoided.

The majority of the companies we examined in this chapter, however, were caught in a crisis as a result of behavior that they believed to be legal and appropriate, a factor that contributed to their being blindsided. Most companies do not have internal scanning processes that enable them to catch public opinion problems before those problems explode and are unprepared when they do.

We have identified a common set of phases from the examples presented in this chapter:

1. A company usually has early warning signals, the implications of which are suppressed.

    Examples of early warning signals include Robins' laboratory results, Union Carbide's safety problems at Bhopal, Nigeria's earlier imprisonment of opposition protesters, and NGO criticisms of apparel manufacturers. Kjistine Anderson of Texaco calls these warnings "signals of dissonance" and told of hearing a clear one herself when a colleague asked her not to use the term "Texaco family" any more, because it wasn't true.

2. Though the crisis itself occurs, either suddenly (Union Carbide in Bhopal) or over a period of time (Shell in Nigeria), the event is almost always described afterward with words such as "inconceivable" or "impossible" and with other language that indicates no existing planning processes had envisioned the possibility of what did, in fact, happen.

3. The company first begins making conscious choices during the immediate reaction phase.

    This period of time is crucial, because important truths about the culture of an organization are revealed when things are moving so fast that people have no time to think before they act. This phase is also the time of maximum news coverage, when the CEO's personal leadership style plays a key role in how the company will be perceived by the public and how employees react. Does the CEO focus on damage control and denial, attack the critics, or concentrate personally on matters that the public feels strongly about (such as any human victims, repairing immediate damage, etc)? Texaco CEO Peter Bijur summarizes what he learned personally from his own time on the firing line: So many daily-level crises arise in the normal course of business operations that it is sometimes difficult to foresee the one that is going to explode. Once it explodes, though, the CEO's task is to deal with it rather than pass it off to someone else. Most important, "follow your instincts: I didn't need advice, I needed help in implementing."

Crisis situations affect more people than just the senior management of a company. A striking feature of our conversations with employees whose companies had experienced a crisis was the intensity of the 48 hours immediately following the initial event. Employees' memories of where and how they first heard the news, their shock and anxiety as the story or rumors of the story unfolded, and their thirst for a clear and immediate message from senior management—these emotions still remain strong no matter how many months or years ago the actual events occurred.

This issue is important for two reasons. First, employee reaction to a crisis (in the short and long term) will have an effect on the company's functioning for a long time afterward. Second, emotional reactions are data. Most managers consider emotional concerns subjective and therefore discount them, but in reality employee reactions are significant signals of what is going on in an organization and should not be ignored. Intense reactions by employees to accusations of wrongdoing illustrates the depth of their need to feel in sync morally with their employer and their need to believe that their employer is in sync with society's norms.

4. Depending on its choices during the initial reaction phase, the company then moves into some combination of damage control, denial/paralysis, and substantively addressing the crisis situation itself. This period of time can be brief or can last for years.

Companies that emerge safely from the crisis tend to be those in which senior management is personally and visibly involved by focusing on substantive responses to the victims or potential victims of the event and by communicating clear direction to employees.

5. Another important choice is finally made when the company settles on its internal evaluation of the crisis.

The answer to the question "What happened to us?" determines the answer to the question "What did we learn?" which goes on to shape the next behavioral cycle of the organization, possibly for years. This change in behavior is largely due to the intense emotional climate within which this process takes place; the learnings that occur are almost literally branded into the brains of the people who weathered the crisis together.

The examples we cited earlier—lessons from the Shell and Texaco cases—were repeated, in various ways, by almost every employee we met.

Studying the process in terms of these phases—warning signals, crisis, immediate reaction, policy change, and development of learnings—may help demonstrate why traditional risk management techniques fail to prepare a company adequately for a crisis; traditional techniques are designed to think the thinkable, not the unthinkable.

4

Risk Management or Scenario Thinking?

Traditional risk management in a corporation tends to gravitate toward thinking about that which can be insured against. It focuses on risks that insurance companies either cover or explicitly refuse to cover and on the proper financial management of those costs and benefits.

If we use the traditional risk management context to look at many of the examples described in the previous chapter, some natural corporate responses become obvious. Boycotts, being impossible to quantify and in most cases undetectable, become scarcely an issue. Product liability, on the other hand, looms huge—partially because of peculiarities of the American legal system and partially because there are established systems for off-loading that risk. Aetna, for example, provided $369 million toward A. H. Robins's liability in the Dalkon Shield case. The very fact that companies routinely carry product liability insurance creates its own form of "moral hazard." Except for cases on a scale that most companies do not ever imagine, the financial consequences to an American company of a normal product liability suit are already budgeted for through its insurance policies. The length of time required to resolve such problems in the courts also helps reduce financial impact, making the net present value of the amounts eventually awarded even smaller.

Other factors in our examples that can be quantified include: the additional cost of the final disposal of the Brent Spar; the cost of Texaco's settlement; the nuisance value of the public relations battles that Nike or Nestlé might have to conduct; and, of course, any direct costs of remedying a problem (such as environmental cleanups or giving contract workers additional wages or benefits). These quantifiable costs are the ones that companies most often think about in advance and in some cases actively prepare and plan for.

The more difficult task for companies is to identify the risk that cannot be quickly or easily quantified—the risk that might nonetheless penetrate straight to the heart of the brand or the business idea. This type of risk (to use an example from another sector) is the one to which the U.S. charity United Way was exposed when its top executive was found to have been misusing funds—the scandal struck directly at the United Way's mission, which was to be a responsible steward of donations intended for the needy of America. Public support and financial contributions plummeted, and the organization had a long fight back to health.

Organizations find it very hard to have conversations about questions such as "What could happen in the future that would put us out of business?" Almost any American company faces the possibility of a product liability suit big enough to put it out of business. A company would benefit from asking itself whether its resources are being directed both at financial protection, that is, building legal firewalls and constructing the best possible insurance coverage, and as important, at production processes designed to pose the least safety risk. Companies whose focus is entirely on the former may be risking their reputation if the unthinkable happens. Public opinion will not easily excuse them for the result, even if the ultimate legal and financial outcome is in their favor (see the Union Carbide and Robins examples in the previous chapter).

Companies that infrequently conduct this in-depth, "what could go badly wrong for our business" type of conversation, especially when things are going well, are even more unlikely to ask themselves more difficult questions (because there are worse things than being put out of business, as we all know when we think about our own children's health and safety). "What could happen in the future that would implicate us—as a company or as individuals—in the suffering or death of human beings?" is such a question. Except in the context of employee health and safety procedures, such questions are not a standard part of the typical company risk management assessment.

Companies that do ask these questions are beginning to move beyond traditional risk management. These questions have made scenario thinking, which enables companies to think more broadly and long term than usual, an increasingly important part of corporate planning. The combination of these techniques (scenario thinking, the business idea, and strategic planning) offers powerful tools for making the risk management process more than an actuarial exercise. The first step is for the company to literally give itself permission to ask these types of questions, that is, for management to set the example by personally acknowledging the importance of such questions.

Scenario thinking can be used in situations that are less dramatic but that still involve serious threats for the company. For example, a flagship product can be reexamined with a hard eye toward what could make that product a negative rather than a positive for the company. Mattel recently took this scenario approach in deciding to do a thorough rethink of one of their most profitable products, the Barbie doll. In the course of the analysis the company realized that despite Barbie's popularity with young girls, the girls' mothers often felt great conflict about their daughters' desire to play with the dolls because of the messages the doll seemed to be conveying about the female ideal. Mattel also discovered that some of its own female employees were embarrassed to tell acquaintances that they were involved with the product. Accurately sensing that this problem could, over time, harm both the product and the brand position, company managers saw a possible future in which mothers would decide that the image of Barbie not only was not cool, but was actually harmful. Mattel managers decided, as a result of the review, to reposition the doll to be a more positive model for girl children and to more accurately reflect mothers' aspirations for their daughters. Their objective was to prevent the negatives that were becoming associated with the doll from causing damage either to product revenues or to the brand image of Mattel itself. Although this situation was not likely to lead to a crisis in the sense we discussed in Chapter 3, it could easily have led to a steady erosion of Mattel's leadership position in the industry and was therefore worth the level of management attention it received.

The Nike Business Idea

As a hypothetical example, let's apply Mattel's thought process to the case of Nike.

Figure 4.1 is an illustration, taken from Kees van der Heijden, of the generic business idea. As mentioned in Chapter 3, the business idea is *not* a mission statement, vision, five-year plan, or new product. The business idea makes it possible for an organization to combine its distinctive competencies to meet a societal need in some unique and hard-to-duplicate way and, by doing so, to generate a positive feedback loop that keeps revenues and resources growing.

Let's define Nike's version of the generic business idea.

1. Evolving needs of society?

Humans clothe themselves for more reasons than just to stay warm. Fashion evolved as part of the human need to decorate, display status, create a persona. Fashion as an industry has traditionally been organized around a target market consisting of adult women who are relatively well-to-do. The emotional needs that the fashion industry meets for this market exist in other, newer markets as well: young people, males, people with less money.

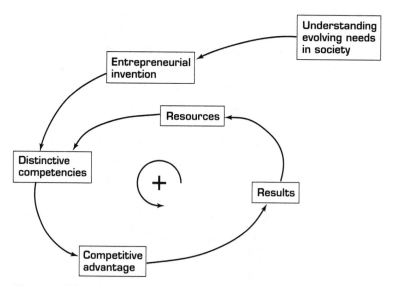

Figure 4.1 The Generic Business Idea

2 Entrepreneurial invention?

Nike presents the sport shoe as fashion: an apparel item that has the potential to become the $100 equivalent, for new young, male markets, of the $5,000 Chanel suit, the item consumers feel they have to have or at least have to aspire to.

3. Distinctive competencies?

What does Nike require in order to make its invention a success? It decides to invest in attractive design and marketing via sports heroes in order to create an image that will add value to the shoe itself, which essentially performs the same function as its competitors' shoes.

4. Competitive advantage?

Nike obtains long-term representation and licensing rights from the era's most popular sports stars, particularly Michael Jordan. Nike makes marketing investments large enough to create a company identification with these stars and therefore portrays the image of a young, energetic, masculine organization, one that is strong and bold enough not to have to follow the rules: Just Do It.

5. Results?

Nike results are market leadership, growing profits, sufficient resources to sustain and strengthen the distinctive competencies, which are ever more expensive endorsements, more product lines, larger geographic reach.

6. Resources?

Nike feeds the positive loop with more heroes, more revenues, more status (Tiger Woods follows Michael Jordan).

What we have presented here can fairly be described as the Nike business idea. What are some of the risks that could break up the positive direction of this system? Some risks that come to mind include:

- Failure to continue design innovations; looking old
- Sport shoes themselves becoming old; replaced by other forms of footwear
- No longer being able to attract the most popular sports stars
- Events that undercut the company image: no longer cool, no longer young, no longer a winner

Notice that this list does not include several important types of business risk: substitute technology (nobody has yet invented a replacement for shoes), product liability (consumers are not likely to sue Nike if they fall down playing basketball), cost squeezes on profit margins (Nike is not a supermarket, nor are raw materials a major part of its cost structure), environmental cleanups (Nike production processes do not discharge toxic chemicals). In fact, the major risks to the Nike business idea are societal: shifts in fashion preferences themselves or damage to the company's heroic image.

At this stage, scenario development could be helpful to Nike. Can the company conceive scenarios for a future in which:

- Sports figures are no longer heroes?
- Sajor sports figures no longer wish to represent Nike?
- Teenagers renounce consumerism?
- Nike's image becomes a marketing negative instead of a positive?

We talked with some California teenagers whose school was experiencing a controversy about a pending contract with Pepsi-Cola and the advertising sponsorship arrangements that the company was seeking. The students expressed their derision in the phrase "walking billboards" as in "companies see students as walking billboards." Is this type of resistance to logomania likely to spread?

Market research, of course, is done and redone by consumer product companies on a nearly constant basis. But if companies do not ask the broadest possible questions or if their questions do not reach to the real business idea, companies will miss the most important kinds of risk.

Finally, let us set aside the Nike example in order to underline the importance of the issue of correctly defining risk by an organization. In Nike's case, the scenario thinking question "Is there a scenario in which the company could be responsible for human suffering or death?" is unlikely to be answered yes. A strike at a contractor factory turning violent? Chinese police shooting demonstrating workers? These risks may appear small compared to those facing chemical, pharmaceutical, or oil companies—whose very production processes involve enormous safety issues, especially in the developing world—but the historical example in Chapter 2 of the Homestead steel mill strike and its permanent impact on Andrew Carnegie's reputation remains a potent one.

5

Best Practice— and Beyond

Companies need to understand: This is your business here—we're not talking theology.
—PAUL SOLMAN

What Is Best Practice?

A company today facing a business problem is more likely to turn to benchmarking, or "best practice," in its efforts to find a solution. This process has come to be regarded as an advance that helps prevent internal inertia from taking over, keeps the company aware of competitive innovation, and helps it bring in fresh air from outside the organization. Understandably, companies faced with the new challenge of developing a social conscience look outside themselves for help in figuring out how to meet this challenge. Unfortunately, guidelines or models are not clearly established for how companies should respond once they do identify a potential threat to their reputations, to their business, or to the lives of stakeholders. Unlike in the environmental field, there are no parts per million or toxicity test result targets to hit. What does constitute best practice in the area of social responsibility? What kind of research can and should a company do into this question?

Once a company begins its inquiries, it will find some discouragement along the way. The area of social responsibility contains a good deal of debate, because companies in different sectors face very different problems and what works for one sector may be irrelevant to another. For consumer products companies, sourcing issues may be key; for example, they must make sure their suppliers do not follow practices (like animal testing) with which their customers disagree. Companies that do their own manufacturing are likely to have environmental issues. In either case, companies need to be concerned about employment conditions in the manufacturing setting: the use of child or bonded labor, living wage levels, collective bargaining rights.

For resource companies, relationships with national governments or state-owned joint venture partners are a major issue. On what terms are those relationships to be agreed? When should the company invest/disinvest and based on what criteria? How should the environmental and developmental rights of surrounding communities, especially in fragile ecosystems like the rain forest, be protected? How should impoverished people's need for economic development be balanced with preservation of their cultures and surroundings?

There are also differences between companies operating abroad, in a wide range of situations, and companies operating in a single country or in a relatively homogenous range of environments. One of the most potentially explosive issues for the international firm is determining how it should interact with the local police, military, or judiciary. In countries with corrupt and/or abusive law enforcement systems, how can companies ensure their own security? How should international companies respond to national discriminatory employment practices like apartheid laws, laws requiring discrimination on the basis of sex, national origin, social status, or other category? Should companies hire women if national legislation prohibits or limits it? Should companies meet or try to exceed national minimum standards for wages and benefits if those standards are too low? What is too low?

And for all companies, how far should or can they go in trying to change or improve social practices in the countries in which they operate? Does an American company have the right to promote free and fair elections in Nigeria? Does a German company have the right to try to eliminate the death penalty in Florida? This last question underlines another important point. Many American companies shy away from questions of social responsibility because they do not feel they have the right to impose American values on the rest of the world. That feeling is particularly valid because, as in the case of our death penalty question, American values do not always look the same abroad as they do at home. In fact, they look a great deal more like plain self-interest than altruism to many nations. Not for nothing (as they say in New York) is the Helms-Burton Act, ostensibly passed in defense of democracy in Cuba, also known as the Bacardi Bill.

On the other hand, as we saw in the discussion of corporate reputation in Chapter 3, companies who practice one set of values at home and another abroad are, these days, as likely to be accused of hypocrisy and exploitative behavior as to be praised for their multiculturalism. In addition, inconsistent practices strike at the heart of the idea of integrity—a company that does not observe what it claims are its core values everywhere will have trouble with credibility in espousing those values anywhere.

A company choosing to think about questions of social responsibility also needs to understand that it does so in the context of a world that has already decided on certain norms. There are international conventions, agreements, and standards to which the over- — not whelming majority of the world's nations have agreed. These agree- so ments provide a starting point for a firm's examination of its own operational obligations. See, for example, the later addenda to the Universal Declaration of Human Rights, the Covenant on Civil and Political and Economic Rights, and the Covenant on Social and Cultural Rights, which provide a general context for the question of best practice; specific protocols such as the United Nations Guidelines for Law Enforcement Officials (which cover use of force, firearms, and other practices involved in security); and other agreements on relevant issues such as the rights of indigenous peoples in development.

Taking these governmental agreements as their starting point, a group of international business leaders known as the Caux Round Table (CRT) adopted in 1995 its own set of standards: the Caux Round Table Principles for Business. The CRT, first meeting in 1986, began as a group of 9 Japanese, 7 American, and 12 European CEOs, although its main driving forces were Ryuzaburo Kaku of Canon and Frederick Philips of Philips Electronics. Kaku's philosophy of *kyosei,* or acting for the common good, and Philips's conviction that "figures are important; people are more important" helped shape the CRT principles. These principles state that corporations have certain responsibilities toward society, such as the following:

- To promote sustainable development
- To promote human rights and democratic institutions wherever practicable

- To collaborate with those in the community who are working to promote health and education
- To be a good corporate citizen

These responsibilities are hard to argue with. The CRT and other business organizations have been trying over the years to bring these responsibilities down to a level of specificity that provides operational guidance for companies who want to give their employees clear, measurable procedures to follow. While at the Tallberg workshop in 1998, Goren Lindahl of ABB said of his employees, "We must be precise if we want 215,000 people to run in the same direction." Problems with specificity arise in defining the terms used in the CRT's principles. Although some progress has been made in identifying forms of "sustainable development," what are "democratic institutions"? Does a multiparty election in which the same (military) candidate intends to represent all five parties, as proposed in Nigeria in 1998, constitute democracy? Most people would say not; but some might say that an election in which a serious candidate has to raise and spend many millions of dollars, as candidates do in the United States, is not a democracy either. When is it "practicable" to defend human rights, and when is it not? The answers to these questions are being developed one company and one situation at a time.

Another approach to the best practice question is to examine those companies whose innovations or practices have already been recognized as socially responsible by some organization or agency. This search for "good" versus "bad" companies is not as easy as it might appear. Indeed, thanks to the very complexity of these questions, a niche has developed within the investment advisory industry—the social investor services. These organizations (some commercial, some nonprofit) provide screening for individual and institutional investors who want to direct their resources toward companies with good records and reputations. In 1995 in the United States, 182 major investing institutions were managing socially responsible investments totaling $639 billion, and that amount is growing rapidly each year. TIAA-CREF, the largest private pension fund in the United States, negotiates directly with corporations about its human rights–related concerns and participates in some shareholder initiatives. With $186 billion in assets, mainly from university faculty and staff across the country, TIAA-CREF is one of the largest holders of shares traded on the New York Stock Exchange.

The management of New York City's pension funds, totaling $62.6 billion, increasingly are questioning the companies they invest in about their conduct in countries with serious human rights violations, and the pension funds support shareholder resolutions asking companies to report on the human rights implications of their operations in Myanmar. The funds managers are discussing an increase in the portion of their assets that are invested in emerging markets funds, and a deciding factor in those investments will be the human rights and labor records of corporations in those developing countries. For corporations doing business in China, for example, the pension funds executives will keep in touch with human rights networks to learn how a particular corporation reacts to labor unrest—does it call in the army, or does it constructively talk with strike leaders?

The Interfaith Center on Corporate Responsibility in New York, a major coordinating body for shareholder activism, has issued its own set of benchmarks for corporate behavior: the Principles for Global Corporate Responsibility, revised and released in 1998. The document also includes 24 separate appendices containing specific conventions and principles ranging from the CERES Principles on the Environment to the Convention on the Rights of the Child to the Advertising Code.

Although these socially aware investors so far are primarily public pension funds, family foundations, and others with particular ethical incentives, the trend is spreading as transparency increases. Individuals can easily go to the Internet Web sites of such organizations as Multinational Monitor or Corporate Watch and read about the activities of international corporations in order to make their own judgments about what investments they want their pension funds or mutual fund managers to support or what shareholder campaigns they can participate in. Nonprofit organizations like Business for Social Responsibility and the Council on Economic Priorities also provide information for tracking performance in this area. Unfortunately for those seeking absolutes, this massive increase in available information only confirms that there are no simple answers to the question of which companies are considered good and which are considered bad. The complexities that emerge in response to this question have been summarized by Dr. Ritchie Lowry of Boston

College in what he calls his Simple Steps and Strategies for Socially Responsible Investing.

According to Dr. Lowry, trying to establish an absolute screen is extremely difficult. For example, an investor who wishes to screen out all inherently polluting companies would avoid pharmaceuticals, even the highly regarded Johnson & Johnson. The absolute approach would also eliminate investing in Procter & Gamble, another well-respected company that has greatly reduced its use of animal testing procedures but still insists that some tests have no viable substitute procedures and therefore some animal testing is necessary in order to protect human users.

Some investors use instead a proportionate impact strategy that assumes, for example, that all energy companies produce a certain level of undesirable environmental impact, and therefore the appropriate screening standard becomes the relative level of impact produced by one company compared to others. Other reviewers look for best practice within an industry or across certain specific functional areas. For example, the Council on Economic Priorities (CEP) gives Corporate Conscience Awards annually to companies for their employee support programs, sourcing practices, community lending or philanthropic programs, or environmentally friendly manufacturing processes. Companies that have received awards from the CEP in recent years include Kellogg, Sainsbury (the British supermarket chain), Wilkhahn, Wilkening (the German furniture manufacturer), Hewlett-Packard, Pfizer Pharmaceuticals, Starbucks, and Fuji Xerox—not for being good companies per se, but for certain programs or practices that the CEP considers worthy of emulating.

The CEP has also recently issued an *International Sourcing Report* based on surveys of 360 companies in up to 40 countries to review compliance with the new SA 8000 sourcing standard. The 1997 four "Top Performers," according to the CEP's methodology, were Toys R Us, Reebok International, Phillips–Van Heusen, and Levi Strauss. In addition, *Fortune* magazine annually rates the world's "most admired" companies. The criteria used in this ranking are innovativeness, ability to attract and retain talented employees, management quality, product quality, value as a long-term investment, financial soundness, community and environmental responsibility, and productive use of assets. (Interesting in light of our discussion of corporate reputation, *Fortune* has established that the single most reliable predictor of overall excellence in a company is the ability to attract and retain talented employees.) In 1997, the three U.S. companies most highly rated for their environmental and community programs were Coca-Cola, Herman Miller, and Corning.

For some people who have participated in the social investment process, the screening exercise has proved of limited value. Paul Hawken, a corporate critic and environmentalist who used to work with the CEP on their awards program, now feels that social investors "haven't even stepped onto the carpet in the room inside the building inside the town where the real issues are." For Hawken, screening of companies may be important as a form of feedback on behavior, but at best is only "a tactic, not a vision." Hawken's own vision is of a world that limits, not encourages, economic growth and financial rates of return—a world in which, for example, companies would not consider doing business with murderous regimes and, if they did, would be ostracized by their peers instead of just screened out of investment portfolios. From this perspective, social investing is a palliative, not a serious critique of corporate behavior.

In terms of feedback on bad behavior, the publication *Multinational Monitor* publishes a list of "Worst Companies" every year—a list with limited validity because it tends to heavily feature resource companies (for reasons noted earlier), companies that have reacted to emerging problems with what the *Monitor* considers defensive or arrogant behavior, and companies that have gotten bad press during the year. It is not always clear, as a result, whether the list is meant to include companies that actually did do the worst things in a given year or just companies that got the most negative publicity for what they did. Some companies receiving this dubious award recently have included Archer Daniels Midland (which turns up on *Fortune's* least admired list), Daishowa, Disney (which turns up on *Fortune's* most admired list), Gerber, Mitsubishi, and Daiwa Bank.

The *Multinational Monitor* example raises another issue, which relates to the second discouragement that companies may encounter in searching for best practice. For many NGOs, the corporate world is monolithic—no distinctions are made between Shell and Unocal, between Nike and Reebok—and as a result, useful opportunities to encourage some initiatives while justifiably criticizing others are lost. Reading NGO material on corporate behavior can lead investors to conclude that companies are seldom, if ever, praised for their efforts—certainly never for trying and failing, or for trying and not succeeding enough. This issue will require rethinking (and reperceiving) by NGOs in future years if they want to increase their effectiveness in bringing about real change in corporate behavior.

So far, our discussions have been about the most general rating organizations, but many more resources, generally NGOs, monitor corporate practice in specialized areas. Business for Social Responsibility, the Interfaith Center on Corporate Responsibility, and other resource centers can act as a guide to these specialized information sources.

In addition to monitoring individual company initiatives and following the work of NGOs that evaluate corporations for social responsibility, managers focusing on issues particular to their own sectors can seek out industrywide initiatives to develop, monitor, and enforce common standards of best practice. An example of such an initiative is the WHO agreement on baby food marketing, which was mentioned in the Chapter 3 discussion of the Nestlé case. A similar initiative is the CEP's sourcing report titled *Social Accountability 8000—A Global Standard for Ethical Sourcing* (SA 8000). According to the CEP, "SA 8000 provides a framework for the independent verification of the ethical production of all goods, made in companies of any size, anywhere in the world." The draft standard was launched for consultation in October 1997. Toys R Us, Avon, and Otto Versand mail order company have committed to adopting the standard, and certification agencies around the world are gearing up to assist companies in achieving compliance.

The context in which the CEP undertook this project was one in which well-intentioned companies were adopting progressive, but often inconsistent, codes of conduct; one in which the challenges of monitoring performance were becoming more obvious; and one in which consumers were increasingly demanding corporate accountability not just for corporations' behavior toward their own employees, but for their contractors' behavior as well. As the ICCR principles state: "The company (should) accept responsibility for all those whom it employs either directly or indirectly through contract suppliers, sub-contractors, vendors or suppliers."

SA 8000 involves auditing companies on a wide range of issues: child labor, health and safety, freedom of association and the right to collective bargaining, discrimination, disciplinary practices, working hours, and most crucially, compensation, that is, wages that meet basic needs. The model for the process will be the current ISO 9000 and ISO 14000 systems. Companies will have incentive to comply with SA 8000. Mail order company Otto Versand has stated that "the costs of not complying with ethical standards will cost more in the long run than will compliance." This view also reflects another incentive: Standards function as a form of level playing field that helps keep costs predictable.

A key feature of the CEP's effort was the diverse nature of its advisory board, which included representatives of NGOs, corporations, unions, accounting firms, and universities. This diversity, in itself, is beginning to emerge as a form of best practice. Companies can seek out diversity of culture and outlook as a form of insurance against blind spots. Interestingly, these consultative processes sometimes present as much of a problem for NGOs as for companies. The thalidomide moral quandary in the previous chapter is a good example; it was as much a violation of organizational norms for the TVA to meet with Celgene as the other way round, and some NGOs are not willing to become involved with companies on a consultative basis. Nonetheless, the TVA and Celgene have concluded that negotiation as well as confrontation is needed to make changes happen on the ground. Examples of diversity are multiplying and will accelerate if the increasing demand for independent verification continues—NGOs will be asked to act as official monitors as well as critics of corporate behavior.

The appendix contains contact information for some of the organizations most deeply involved in identifying, developing, and disseminating corporate experience in social responsibility. However, in terms of the best practice debate, it is important for companies to understand not only that the models of the future are yet to be developed but that the models of the future may not be models at all in the sense we have understood them in the past. In fact, the quest for a model may represent a serious detour for a company wishing to address the question of social responsibility. Why? Because, with the speed of change in today's world, by the time a company has identified and locked into a particular mental model of the way something works, the model is likely to be already out of date. Shell certainly thought its original Statement of General Business Principles represented a behavioral model that would last intact for as long as its current management could imagine—and then learned the hard way that even the best models must be updated to reflect new thinking and conditions. A company's goal has to be, in the end, not discovery of a model of social responsibility but development of a process that will create its own, living understanding of its place in the wider world. This goal means asking hard questions and thinking even harder about the answers—constantly. Companies that are rule followers, in a world in which the rules are changing, are the ones most at risk.

If our discussion of models seems to imply that codes of conduct and other statements of corporate values are not sufficient measures of social responsibility, the impression is accurate. Almost every company has such a statement. The real issue is how that statement translates operationally; what the baseline of performance is, and then how progress against that baseline is monitored. The ICCR's principles document reflects this concern by including, for each principle outlined, both criteria and benchmarks for determining whether the principle has in fact been implemented. See the boxed text for an example.

The London Benchmarking Group and specialized consulting firms such as the Corporate Citizenship Company have begun developing auditable standards in such areas as a template for defining corporate community involvement, environmental standards, and work practices. For the Hitachi Foundation, the Corporate Citizenship Company prepared an exhaustive report (building on earlier work by one of its authors, David Logan, a former Levi Strauss executive) on international corporate support for community development. The report, published in 1997, presents a remarkable picture of the changing focus of corporate philanthropy. Emphasis is shifting increasingly from cash donations, divorced from strategic business needs, toward investing in long-term relationships with the broader community, based on similarly long-term company interests.

Some specific examples from the Hitachi Foundation report include: partnerships between American Express and Share Our Strength (an NGO fighting world hunger); Hong Kong's Private Sector Committee on the Environment; Philippine Business for Social Progress; the Prince of Wales Business Leaders Forum in the United Kingdom; Land O'Lakes's trading initiative with indigenous peoples in Chiapas, Mexico; British American Tobacco's policy of

Joint Ventures/Partnerships/Subsidiaries

Principles

When entering into and throughout the duration of joint ventures and partnerships, the company takes into account the ethical implications as well as the financial implications of those relationships.

All parts of the company, associated companies, divisions and units and subsidiary companies abide by the same code of ethics and conduct as the parent company as a minimum standard.

The company accepts a responsibility to promote its codes of ethics and of conduct with licensees and franchisees.

Criteria

The company recognizes that unethical behavior by joint venture and other partners reflects on its own reputation and integrity, and the company has a mechanism to address such unethical behavior.

The company has a clearly stated policy in regard to the monitoring of the application of codes of ethics and conduct by licensees and franchisees.

Benchmarks

The company has guidelines to assess and determine its course of action when a violation of ethical codes is perpetrated by a partner or subsidiary. These guidelines include, but are not limited to, challenging the partner or terminating the relationship.

The company takes immediate steps to address violations of codes of ethics and conduct by licensees and franchisees. The company only terminates the relationship as a last resort.

---

sourcing its tobacco in Kenya from small farmers rather than its own large plantations; Levi Strauss's anti-AIDS projects; and IBM's initiative on Social Exclusion, Technology, and the Learning Society, intended to find new ways to use technology in training excluded groups in Europe. The report also cites an extensive effort by British Petroleum to manage the social impacts of plant closures in South

Wales, an effort that involved creation of a $2.5 million economic development agency to attempt to create 700 new jobs to replace the ones lost in the closures. Eight years later, the agency had attracted to the area firms that provided employment for 600 and had allowed existing local companies to retain another 1,600. These examples all illustrate what the authors of the Hitachi Foundation report call "strategic social investment, defined as engaging in the development and maintenance of healthy, vital communities and people as necessary prerequisites for successful business." In addition to our previous examples, we are including here an extensive excerpt from a field research report prepared by Christopher Avery, an international human rights lawyer who visited companies in southeast Asia and South Africa in 1996–1997 to learn what both national and multinational companies were discovering through their work in community development. Avery's research report, together with the Hitachi Foundation report, provides a fascinating overview of emerging best practice in corporate community programs outside the United States. These reports describe the experiments that companies are conducting and the possibilities and problems the companies are encountering in the process. Here is what the Avery report had to say:

Nakornthon Bank works with villagers in northeast Thailand. M. L. Parnuthat Sooksawasd describes the project: "I manage the main branch of Nakornthon Bank in Bangkok. We got involved with this project through a program called Thai Business Initiative in Rural Development... their development experts helped us throughout.

"Before the project began, this village was very poor: rice farming was not providing enough income, children were malnourished, young people left their children with grandparents and migrated to cities to earn money, some women left to work as prostitutes to support their families. In other words, the village was dying economically and socially.

"We didn't impose anything on the villagers... we started by asking them what they saw as their development priorities. Water and electricity were top of the list, so our bank met with government officials and arranged for wells and electricity. Next we worked with villagers to build a sewage system, then a school.

Many of us from the bank go there on weekends and work alongside the villagers.

"Then came the big question: How could the village become economically self-sufficient? We found agricultural experts to identify new activities suited to the soil and climate, and to train the villagers. Dairy cattle, soybeans, corn, organic farming and fruit trees were introduced. We found a dairy consortium to buy the milk. We trained villagers in basic money management and marketing.

"Our approach to everything was not to give charity or create dependency: the villagers did the work and purchased everything—the toilets, the cows, the seeds. We provided low-interest loans to be paid off when they started earning income.

"The results? Income levels skyrocketed. Families reunited as people returned to work in the village. The payoff rate for loans was 100%, and our bank now has a loyal base of customers. The project has been a commercial success for the bank. The project has been so successful that development agencies and the government keep asking me how it was done. I tell them it was done mainly by the villagers themselves."

When Bata Shoe Company needed to expand its operations in Thailand, it worked with development experts from Thai Business Initiative in Rural Development and set up small shoe factories right in poor villages of northeast Thailand. Village cooperatives own and manage these factories, and invest profits to develop their community. Bata provided the training in manufacturing and business skills. The result: villagers returning from Bangkok to self-reliant villages. And these small factories turn out some of the highest quality shoes of any Bata factory in the world, with very healthy profits for Bata.

Bengt Gunnarsson, Managing Director, speaks about these Bata factories in the northeast province of Buri Ram: "We are very proud and we feel very good about the developments in Buri Ram. Today we have an employment of almost 500 people in the province, and this has obviously boosted the economy and helped tremendously the development of many villages there."

Tata, the largest corporate group in India, employs some of the best and brightest development experts to manage its community projects. Tata projects reach thousands of villages throughout

India, including isolated tribal communities. The focus is on promoting self-reliance:

- New methods of agriculture and new crops
- Vocational training
- Income generating projects
- Literacy and health programs

Tata is even installing solar energy devices in villages that have no electricity and where wood is scarce. A Tata company was one of the first in the world to commission an independent social audit of its contributions to society...and it made the audit public.

Companies are also linking up with legal and human rights experts to build civil society and promote the rule of law: Shell Oil in South Africa helped the Community Law Centre publish materials in Zulu and English to help rural people in Kwazulu Natal and the Eastern Cape understand their rights under the new Constitution and Bill of Rights.

In Thailand some companies are supporting Pollwatch, the independent organization trying to ensure fair elections and stop vote-buying by politicians.

In the Philippines, Ayala Corporation is backing an important initiative: human rights experts training a local human rights officer in each community. These neighbourhood human rights officers help people at the grassroots level learn about and protect their rights under the Bill of Rights, and help resolve conflicts by mediation and conciliation. The program is also backed by the national Commission on Human Rights and the Philippines Government.

Carlos Medina, law professor and Director of the Ataneo Law School Human Rights Center which is helping to implement this program; explains that one component is human rights training of the police: "The training of policemen will include focusing on the rights of victims, and also the duties of policemen when they carry out arrests, searches, seizures or detention."

Carlos Medina refers to Ayala's role as a partner in the human rights initiative: "We are fortunate enough to work with Ayala Foundation, because Ayala Foundation provides for the resources while we have the expertise, so that way it's like a team. We work together promoting human rights down at the grass-roots level."

Philip Balie speaks about how Levi Strauss Corporation is seeking to contribute to the new South Africa: "looking at encouraging within this country a culture of human rights, and looking at areas where there is violence and where deeds of the past have left trauma." Levi Strauss is supporting a trauma centre for victims of violence and torture, as well as a training facility for Cape Town's street children.

The four founders of The Plan Group, 14 Thai companies known for their business success and social responsibility, were students in the 1970s. They lived under a military government and saw their fellow students killed on the streets by the security forces. They resolved they would use their business careers to make a difference in their country. They encourage all employees to help conceive, plan and implement the Group's extensive community and environmental projects.

One of those projects is described [again, paraphrased from the original] by Pafun Supavanich: "When the Plan Group recognized the need for radical improvement of Thailand's education system, we decided to start a model school. We commissioned the country's best education experts to design a dynamic curriculum and a new approach to teaching. That school has been a resounding success, and the government is drawing lessons from the school on how the country's education system can be reformed."

Hindustan Lever, the Indian division of Unilever, started its development project as a business necessity. In 1975 the company almost had to close its commercial dairy in Etah, because even though the local villagers had plenty of cows, they weren't producing much milk. The company found that low milk productivity was only a symptom. The problem: villagers lived in such a state of poverty that they could not afford to feed or care for their animals properly. In 1976 Hindustan Lever embarked on a long-term Integrated Rural Development Program in the area. They have worked with 600 villages toward self-sufficiency.

The result: a marked improvement in the lives, health and income levels of the rural people. The villagers are now loyal consumers of Hindustan Lever products. And the dairy? It is now operating at full capacity, with plans for expansion.

There's another dimension to this story. Since 1979 Hindustan Lever has required its management trainees to leave their plush offices in India's cities and spend two months living and working with the villagers in Etah, participating in the development process. In addition to the contribution made by the trainees, the corporation feels that its future managers are getting a first-hand understanding of rural India, which after all is the main market for Hindustan Lever's products. This is the best type of innovation—the kind that perpetuates and reproduces itself, enabling employees to experiment and develop still more forms of innovative behavior—a true distinctive competency.

Anglo-American (South Africa's largest company, the world's number 1 in the mining industry) manager Margie Keeton notes that the company's attitude toward social responsibility was shaped by the man who founded the company in 1917, Sir Ernest Oppenheimer: "He said that it was the duty of the corporation to make profits for its shareholders, but to earn them in such a way as to make a real and permanent contribution to the well being of the people and to the development of Southern Africa."

Anglo-American supports some very large projects in rural development, education and community health—but also makes more than 1,000 grants per year to small, grassroots initiatives.

The company's philosophy is that it should not only support tried and tested programs: "We do believe in taking risk and encouraging innovation, looking for the pioneering initiatives, if you like, the projects which (to use a boxing metaphor) fight above their weight. We look for people who are trying to do new and different things, and then we back them in the belief that the success of one pioneering initiative will be that much greater than simply doing what others have done before."

Eunice Sibiya, Community Affairs Manager at Coca-Cola Southern Africa, states: "The company focuses on education, because the company believes that to succeed we need an educated society." In one project, Coca-Cola assisted an impoverished community in the East Rand:

"Children of about 6 or 7 years old had to walk 10 to 15 kilometres to the nearest school. The informal settlement occupied by half a million people had become a very big community overnight with no social facilities and amenities, no shops, no schools, nothing. We were approached by the community with about 600 signatures saying can you please provide a school for that community."

Coca-Cola came up with a novel, cost-effective solution: a shipping company donated a big shipping container, Coca-Cola worked with the community to build a foundation and convert the container into a school, and Coca-Cola arranged with the government for provision of teachers.

HDFC, a leading Indian financial corporation, makes low-interest loans to promote home ownership among the weaker sectors of society. It is also looking at ways to strengthen micro-credit institutions that support small-scale enterprise.

Nasser Munji of HDFC: "In a country like India, the opportunities for directing credit to where it's most needed on a commercially viable basis can achieve the twin objectives of social development as well as commercial viability, and if you can do both, then you have sustainable development."

In Northern Thailand around the Nan River, native forests are at risk. Here a reforestation project is underway...a special project, because it brings together four partners: private sector companies, development organizations, the government, and most importantly the local hill tribe people themselves.

Paiboon Wattanasiritham is president of the Thailand Rural Reconstruction Movement, a development organization involved in this reforestation project. He is also an economist, former President of the Thai Stock Exchange, and a member of Parliament. He describes one of the TRRM's projects: "The Community Forestry Project involves the training of hill tribe people to better manage their resources and their environment.

"The project fully involves hill tribe people in all stages of planning and implementation. The goal is to support and strengthen the hill tribe people as a community, because they are the best stewards of the forest.

"The reforestation helps the hill tribe people to be more conscious, more aware, more committed, to preventing deforestation, to protecting the natural environment, and when they do that of course they benefit because when the environment is better the water flows better, the soil becomes more fertile, there are richer resources from the forest, for example, they can go into the forest, they can go and pick mushrooms, they can pick bamboo shoots, they can benefit from the herbs.

"They of course benefit also from working together as a community. They are more conscious of social well-being. They think more about the welfare of their children. So the community as a whole becomes better not only in economic but also in social terms."

Bangchak Petroleum in Thailand helps rural people form co-operatives to own and manage for themselves petrol stations, tanker trucks, and small markets selling organic foods and local handicrafts. The company provides the business skills training, guarantees the loans, sells the gasoline wholesale to the cooperatives, and works with development specialists to build the capacity of local communities. This program brings greater self-sufficiency to over 500 farming communities, over 1 million families. It also has been extremely profitable for Bangchak Petroleum, one of Thailand's most successful companies.

Sophon Suphapong, President of Bangchak Petroleum said recently: "In the past 30 to 40 years, business is the only sector that has grown strong while [rural] people have become poorer and the government sector weaker. It is essential business gives [opportunity] to society. The world's market just won't buy products if they are manufactured by countries that exploit child labour; that are dictatorial; and that destroy the environment. Business [people] have no choice but to take part in the process of resolving our social problems."

Christopher Avery summarizes his experience by stating, "All these projects demonstrate what a difference companies can make when they set their mind to it, and when they approach community projects with the same professionalism, creativity and commitment as their core business. None of these companies is giving more than it can afford or sacrificing its bottom-line. In fact, they profit handsomely from these projects, sometimes in direct monetary terms, always by enhancing the company's reputation. And the best and brightest employees today want to work for a respected company that plays its part in society...Unfortunately, these companies and projects are more the exception than the rule."

Even programs such as the ones Avery mentions can fall victim to the Carnegie syndrome—in terms of reputation, all the donated libraries in the world may fail to make up for one Homestead strike (see Chapter 2). And, as we discuss later, these projects do not address a basic demand increasingly being made of companies by their host communities: security of employment, or preservation of jobs in the face of globalization.

We close this section with a look at U.S. companies who enjoy strong reputations for their responsibility. We look at The Body Shop, Ben & Jerry's, Levi Strauss & Company (mentioned earlier), and Hewlett Packard (also one of Fortune's most admired companies).

The Body Shop (TBS) was founded by Anita and Gordon Roddick, whose personal commitments to social concerns have now created a culture that attracts and supports employees with similar values. TBS was also one of the first companies to initiate ethical audits (the first was published in 1995). These audits were a precursor of the independent monitoring and verification process, a concept that is not limited only to consumer businesses. As Richard Boele, campaigns manager for TBS, stated, "That's what's radical and groundbreaking—that TBS allowed the public to evaluate what the company does." Another TBS practice that Boele feels is going to be taken up by other companies is corporate campaigning. Boele's definition of corporate campaigning is "reversing the long tradition of getting involved in campaigning only to increase or protect profits" and conducting campaigns to improve community health standards, reduce corruption, and other social benefits.

Ben & Jerry's, the United States ice cream manufacturer, demonstrates the same connection between its founders' values and its corporate practice. Founder Ben Cohen, at a workshop on Business for Social Transformation in 1993, described the following situation. The company has historically relied on small local dairy farmers as suppliers. The price differential between milk from those suppliers and industrial-sized dairy farms rose substantially. The company had to decide whether to switch contracts. The decision was made to stay with the (temporarily) more expensive family farms, according to Cohen, for two reasons: the commitment that Ben & Jerry's had made to support sustainable agriculture and the desire to maintain consistent relationships with suppliers as a method of keeping prices down over the long term. He estimated that the choice cost the company in the neighborhood of $100,000, a sum they could scarcely afford to lose at that point. The company has also made a practice of sourcing from sustainable agriculture cooperatives in developing countries and making shop franchises available to local entrepreneurs in ordinarily uninvestable communities.

Levi Strauss (LS & Co), which has recently contributed to the creation of a new Resource Center for Corporate Responsibility jointly with Business for Social Responsibility, uses the phrase "responsible commercial success" to describe its promise to shareholders. The linkage Levi Strauss sees between values and business success is stated succinctly by its chairman and CEO, Robert Haas: "A company's values—what it stands for, what its people believe in—are crucial to its competitive success." Levi Strauss communicates its values to its employees through its Aspirations Statement and its CORE Curriculum—documents that function as an expanded code of conduct for the organization. An example of the guidelines that Levi Strauss provides to employees are the following communication guidelines for marketing:

- First and foremost, use common sense.
- Celebrate people's strength, don't prey on their weaknesses.
- Always judge the messaging of our advertising from the eyes of our consumers.
- Learn to embrace diversity.
- Be genuine in all your cause- or issue-related efforts to connect with our customers.
- Never use graphic violence or sex to sell our products.
- Never mislead anyone about our products, period.
- Take the time to understand the difference between a portrayal and a stereotype.
- When evaluating your work, seek a diverse point of view to make sure it reflects diversity.
- Be willing to take risks when our leadership values align with the truths of our consumers.
- Whenever possible, add value to our consumers' lives.
- Last, be responsible but not afraid.

Levi Strauss's reputation for integrating these and similar principles into its business is based on its record of monitoring and enforcing implementation of those principles, for example, by requiring positive employment practices from its contractors overseas. In addition, many of Levi Strauss's country subsidiaries provide financial support and sponsorship for local social justice and health initiatives, through either the activities of the Levi Strauss Foundation or the company itself.

Hewlett-Packard (HP) is another company that takes pride in its strong culture of responsibility, often called the HP Way. HP has developed a set of values and objectives that have served as a unifying force for the company as its strategies and practices change, inevitably, over time. One of these objectives is "Citizenship: to honor our obligations to society by being an economic, intellectual, and social asset to each nation and each community in which we operate." An HP executive explained to us the company's commitment to social responsibility: "The business ecology, like the natural ecology, needs weeds as well as trees. Companies that cut corners, go for the short-term, are welcome to it, but we intend to be a tree and not a weed."

An important way in which HP's principles become integrated into operational practice is in making investment decisions about product development projects. If several different proposals are competing for research funding, the ones most likely to be funded are not necessarily the ones with the greatest financial payback, but those that potentially make the greatest contribution. These types of codes and principles, of course, exist in almost every company. They are often cited when questions of social responsibility arise. The credibility of such codes and company reputation depend ultimately on whether the company holds true to these principles when faced with a crisis or, in the Levi Strauss definition of integrity, when "confronted by personal, professional and social risks, as well as economic pressures."

Beyond Best Practice

The examples cited by Avery, and the Levi Strauss and HP examples, lead toward an important conclusion: that much of the work being done by corporations in terms of social responsibility is not being driven by codes, agreements, or legislation. It is being driven by the operational interests and needs of thoughtful, moral executives themselves who are given encouragement to act responsibly when faced with difficult decisions. As HP's statement of values puts it: "As a practical matter, ethical conduct cannot be assured by written policies and codes; it must be an integral part of the organisation, a deeply ingrained tradition that is passed from one generation of employees to another."

The programs that these companies initiate are developed in collaboration with other stakeholders who can help the company work out the best approaches to the problem. This work is often done very quietly—without public announcements, statements, or position papers. Companies have several reasons for keeping quiet:

1. Many of the programs are highly experimental; the participants know how high the risk of failure is and don't want to take credit for something prematurely.
2. Companies are leery of publicity in these areas anyway. Calling attention to something positive they are doing in one area may only attract criticism of weaknesses elsewhere.
3. NGOs often feel that they maintain their own credibility from criticizing, not from praising, company initiatives. As a result, some NGOs are not as active in searching out positive aspects as they are in finding aspects to campaign against. Companies may have the impression that they will be criticized no matter what they do or how much effort they make.

Despite these obvious disincentives, more and more companies are trying to identify ways in which they can develop a social conscience and then demonstrate that conscience in practice. These operations-oriented initiatives are the ones that we feel are likely to lead to the most productive and sustainable programs. How does a company develop such programs if there is really no best practice model out there to work from? The first step is reperceiving, otherwise known as "unlearning what you already know that isn't true," and we explore this step in the next chapter.

6
Reperceiving Social Responsibility

I've always believed that the greatest contribution a business could make to society was its own success, which is a fountainhead of jobs, taxes, and spending in the community. I still believe that—but I don't think that is enough anymore. And I don't believe that even generous financial philanthropy on top of that prosperity is enough. In these times, companies [cannot] remain aloof and prosperous while surrounding communities decline and decay.
—Jack Welch, Chairman, General Electric

We all pay for poverty and unemployment and illiteracy. If a large percentage of society falls into a disadvantaged class, investors will find it hard to source skilled and alert workers; manufacturers will have a limited market for their products; criminality will scare away foreign investors, and internal migrants to limited areas of opportunity will strain basic services and lead to urban blight. Under these circumstances no country can move forward economically and sustain development.
—Jaime Zobel de Ayala, Chairman of Ayala Group, largest company in the Philippines

In this chapter, we suggest ways of reperceiving the issue of social responsibility, describe techniques for incorporating these perceptions into ongoing company planning and decision-making processes, and encourage careful thinking about risk ahead of time. In short, we outline positive strategies for keeping control of the company's sense of self—its structure, strategy, and options in the new, more demanding future we expect to inhabit.

From our participation in scores of conferences and conversations about corporate social responsibility, we have found that most of us bring heavy baggage to this issue in the form of deep-seated and often unquestioned assumptions. Our main concern in this chapter is to identify and analyze the common assumptions that make it difficult for people in corporations to engage with this issue productively.

One common view, most prevalent in the United States, is that the corporation does stand apart from society and functions best when it gets back to basics, when it is freed of government regulation and constraints and discards social engineering in favor of just plain engineering. This view is, at its root, the argument that shareholder value is the only value that matters. This summary is an oversimplification, but one that certainly was part of the mood of triumphalism that followed the collapse of the Soviet economy. To much of the corporate world, the message of that collapse was that the market, as defined by largely American rules, had won.

Unfortunately for the triumphalists, the issues that sparked Marxism as a social force in the first place—people's inherent desire for justice, fairness, and a secure place in the world for their children—did not go away when state socialism did, but are instead assuming new forms. In addition, we human beings created large organizations—corporations, churches, countries—because we believe that they offer us opportunities to achieve our goals in ways that will survive our own individual lifetimes. Over time, many of those organizations—commercial and noncommercial—have failed humanity in large and small ways. Our history is therefore a record of centuries of effort to improve or reform *something:* our church, our government, our factory, our farm, our family. The modern corporation is no exception to this process and should not claim to stand apart from it or insist on interpreting it in the narrowest possible view.

This discussion of our view leads directly to one of several assumptions that we try to clear away in this chapter: the myth that corporations today can choose whether to become involved with social issues like economic development, diversity and equal opportunity, corruption in government, or human rights. We could name several companies that have, clearly, chosen to involve themselves: The Body Shop and Ben & Jerry's, for example, come to mind. These companies may not be regarded by many in the corporate community as mainstream—Their social responsibility is viewed primarily as part of their marketing mix, or their customer demographics are too narrow, or their founders have particular agendas that set them apart from the rest of the business world. The experience and practice of these two companies are nonetheless very instructive. Both, for example, illustrate clearly the importance of founders' values in establishing corporate values. Most other companies would describe themselves as *not* having made the choices that The Body Shop and Ben & Jerry's did but as having chosen instead to use their resources to satisfy the needs of their customers and create wealth for their shareholders.

The foundation that gives companies the freedom to accomplish these economic goals, however, is the entire infrastructure of civil society—the written and unwritten rules, laws, and protections that most of us have stopped noticing (until we are shocked, in unfamiliar environments, by their absence). The benefits that business receives from this infrastructure imply certain responsibilities in return: for example, transparency, honoring of contracts, and respect for the institutions of the larger society.

Let's look at this concept on a practical level. As soon as a company hires an employee or files a tax return or makes a capital investment, it has involved itself with social issues—it has just not made those involvements explicit. The company pays its employees what the market will bear—*or a little more or a little less*. It enforces certain health and safety practices—*to the minimum required by law or a little better*. It recruits and promotes employees—on the basis of merit, *with fewer or more exceptions for internal or external politics*. The dailiness and familiarity of all these decisions should not be allowed to lull us into thinking that they do not involve big issues. Taken together, they form the life of a corporation in the same way that an individual's daily decisions add up, at some point, to a life. Sooner or later even a corporation, like an individual, needs to ask itself: What kind of history have we created? What sort of legitimacy do we need to endure or succeed? How do we want to be remembered? What is our legacy? Management is increasingly discovering that these questions are on the minds of all employees. Internal trust and support is becoming a major incentive for responsible behavior on the part of corporations, in order to both retain and attract the highest quality workforce.

Another assumption that people often make is to say "Society has changed the rules on us. They used to say we shouldn't get involved with governments, now they say we should." The underlying point of the anti–economic imperialism arguments of earlier years was not simply that firms were interfering with governments' legitimate authority, but that they were doing so out of their own self-interest—and that corporate self-interest was harming workers, the environment, the citizenry. The apparently contradictory demand from some stakeholders that firms now attempt to impose values on certain governments is actually making the same point, that is, in situations in which governments are themselves harming workers, the environment, or the citizenry, company reluctance to challenge those abuses may be equally self-interested and equally harmful.

Countries that have concluded that socialism is dead have a new and generally more positive view of multinational corporations. But companies that are invited in to help create wealth have to accept new responsibilities as part of its role in the economic development process. Accepting these responsibilities is not now seen as intervention by many governments but as part of a legitimate partnership with their citizens (see Nelson Mandela's comments in Chapter 7).

Another assumption made by businesses is that solving social problems is the government's job. Business's job is making a profit and earning returns for its shareholders. Milton Friedman of the University of Chicago has frequently observed: "The social responsibility of business is to maximize its profits." Yes, and... because both of us have worked in planning departments of large organizations, we can vouch for the fact that this statement is, in reality, much less precise and focused than it sounds. When the head of a business unit states that his or her mission is to maximize something—throughput, cargo, net revenues—that person should be sent back to the spreadsheet. Profit targets always represent a choice among many alternative uses of funds—a balancing act that involves inevitable trade-offs and many different possible outcomes.

By treating the income statement of your corporation as a computer simulation, you could maximize profits by paying everyone in the company the lowest possible wage, using the lowest cost raw materials you could find and still meet your quality standards, eliminate all employee benefits not absolutely necessary for recruitment, limit research and development only to those projects with guaranteed commercial applications, and close down your philanthropic programs. Obviously, these aspects are not the basis on which decisions are made, largely because no time frame is specified. Over what period are profits to be maximized? A quarter? A year? Ten years? The more long term an organization's goals are, the less meaning maximizing has. As one CEO has stated, "Social responsibility is very much a question of long-term viability of a business."

One of the most important aspects of long-term viability, as *Fortune's* analysis of most-admired companies has shown, is the quality of employees that the company can recruit. If the brightest young people choose not to work for a particular company because of its negative reputation, this development can damage company performance for years. In addition, although it is true that the particular function of business in society is wealth creation, that function never occurs in a vacuum. Businesses create wealth in the context of particular tax policies, educational policies, judicial practices—all part of creating an environment in which business can operate effectively. The assumption of an exclusive focus on profits may therefore appear to hold true in the short term, but if examined in a long-term perspective, the integrated, systemic nature of the relationship between government and business becomes more obvious.

We can look to the former Soviet Union for a real-world example of why social problems are not something only for governments to worry about. A major reason for the economic crisis in Russia is that civil society and the rule of law have so far failed to develop there. In a training program that one of us ran in St. Petersburg during the early days of liberalization (1993–1996), our best-attended course was always the one on Russian taxation. At these sessions, accountants and attorneys from the top western firms vied with one another at the podium to try to explain the almost indescribable level of chaos and unpredictability of the system that their Russian clients were dealing with. They vied with each other to top the latest outrageous story of a corporation fleeced, an edict rescinded the day it was issued, and other ridiculous features of the tax landscape. The only fixed point seemed to be the stolidly repeated statements by local tax officials that Moscow expected customs duties to produce 25 percent of national income and that they would meet that goal with or without any rational laws or regulations in place.

Another feature of this early period of foreign investment in Russia was that so few western firms were yet making any profits that the government initiated forms of taxation specifically designed to siphon off pretax revenues as well. Because western firms in 1993 paid their employees salaries that were approximately 10 times what employees of Russian organizations received, a tax was imposed on "excess wages." (We used to calculate during these years in St. Petersburg that the reason investors were slow to enter Russia was arithmetically obvious: The tax authorities demanded roughly 60 percent of profits and organized crime another 50 percent.)

Things became even worse for some western companies a few years later when their joint ventures actually began making money. The western partners were often told that they were no longer needed and were, if they were lucky, bought out. If they were not lucky, they could be beaten up, killed, or simply told to leave the country before such accidents might happen to them. For entrepreneurial Russians without the protection of money and somewhere to flee to, starting a small business during that time was even more dangerous. One acquaintance, a woman who started an import-export firm with her husband and son, saw them both hacked to death at the door of their flat by thugs who thought they kept dollars in their home because of their trading activity. She herself was left for dead, but lived. She never thought of going to the public safety system for justice — that would have only exposed her to more risk. In such a climate, is it any wonder that economic growth proved elusive? In such a climate, is it really possible for a business to say that social problems are none of its concern?

Instituting and maintaining civil society — internationally as well as domestically — is clearly as vital to business as it is to private individuals, to church leaders, or to government officials. Civil society is the only way for a society to grow and develop, and no nation can have a civil society without the active support of business. This statement leads us to the next assumption: Western countries should not try to impose their social values on the rest of the world.

In Chapter 5, we discussed the existence of international norms that companies can subscribe to, which negates this assumption. This assumption also becomes harder to sustain if the focus is kept on core human rights issues like due process of law, freedom of conscience, freedom from torture, and freedom from abuse of government power. Cultures around the world share these core values in some form. In addition, culture is not static. Chapter 2 demonstrated that slavery was for centuries a commonly held cultural value in many parts of the world, but that was no reason to perpetuate it indefinitely. Similarly, female genital mutilation and other traditional practices that have harmful effects on women are still common in many societies, but these practices have come under attack from women's organizations and human rights groups in those countries and may well be eliminated in coming years.

Companies are participants, not passive observers, in this process of determining cultural values. A company must do the time-consuming and difficult homework of determining, as far as is possible, what its shared values are and then give employees the tools to act on those values—tools such as clear guidelines, policies, and management support—when they find themselves in a situation of conflict. This process is the unifying force that HP refers to when it speaks of its corporate values.

A related assumption is that doing business in countries with repressive governments is best for the people because in the long run international trade relations will force liberalization. This assumption is Unocal's major public premise. But every company does have a bottom line in terms of where it will operate. If its employees are at physical risk, if it is impossible to avoid participation in policies that the firm considers illegal or immoral, most companies at some point will make a choice not to remain. The question is, where is that line drawn and why? The solution cannot be found until serious internal work is done and until measurable standards are developed. If a company insists that its presence in a country is going to improve a difficult situation, then it needs to gather and publish information that the rest of the world can use to measure accountability: Exactly what does the company expect to improve, and how will those improvements be verified? This kind of baseline study is what Statoil, the Norwegian oil company, performs in the context of its work in problematic countries.

As we discuss later in this chapter, the problem of operating in countries with repressive governments is one of the most complex problems that businesses face. For some companies, the difficulties are just not worth the economic benefit. Other companies may stay because of economic reasons or because they believe the situation will improve; under almost every circumstance, though, the company can expect to be burdened with guilt by association from some segment of the public. One small example: At a recent GBN conference, a young African-American disc jockey was describing how hip-hop became a billion-dollar industry, its images increasingly taken up by mainstream consumer product companies. He cited the example of a particular advertising campaign for Sprite beverage that featured footage of early performances on the streets of New York. When asked if the advertising made him partial to the product as a result, he replied without hesitation, "Sprite is owned by Coca-Cola, and my family is from South Africa. I will never drink a Coke."

International trade's inherently liberalizing qualities may in certain circumstances improve an unstable situation, but not always— especially when the instability results in part from corruption and misuse of the gains of trade. Arguments made by many companies ring truer when the wealth being created is being returned to employees or communities in the form of genuine investment. Too often, such returns are not the case, and the wealth created by foreign investment ends up instead finding a home in Swiss bank accounts (see our discussion of corruption, below).

Finally, one of the most common assumptions is that the groups who criticize businesses are either political radicals with their own agendas or idealists who don't understand how the world works. This assumption, of course, can easily be true in a particular case. But many companies make the leap from a particular reality into the trap of believing that nothing an opponent says can be true or worth thinking about. Reading the position papers of the barbarians at the gates may turn out to be a company's best inoculation against "group-think" and is a key aspect of the reperceiving necessary to address questions of social responsibility. Celgene, for example, spent a year studying the position papers of the Thalidomide Victims Association before approaching them to discuss its project. (Randy Warren: "We should have been the first ones they talked to.")

Talking and dialogue do need to result in some kind of real change, at least in understanding, to be worthwhile. We are aware of several instances in which companies did reach out to NGOs, were warned of emerging problems, and then for various reasons were not able or chose not to act on those warnings. In at least one case, the failure to act resulted in front-page criticism a year later and in possible scuppering of a major business acquisition.

The assumptions we have outlined here can be summarized in the context of the generic business idea. If we include the topic of social responsibility in the business idea graphic, the feedback loop would look like the illustration in Figure 6.1. Social responsibility is a set of add-ons to the business idea and is generally treated as added costs that depress the business results; in other words, social responsibility is a public relations issue.

We are proposing that social responsibility be reperceived as arising from stakeholder responsibility, in which stakeholders such as consumers, employees, governments, shareholders, and local commu-

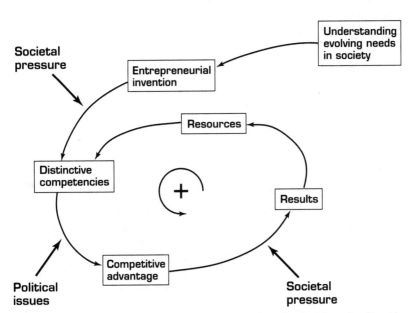

Figure 6.1 If Corporate Responsibility Is Perceived as Coming from the Outside, Company Reaction Will Be Defensive and May Assume Damage to Its Business Idea

nities have the power to push the dynamics of the business idea into either a virtuous or a vicious circle. This analysis would allow a company to broaden its view of social needs, to identify potential new entrepreneurial opportunities arising from those needs, and to begin building the new distinctive competencies that will be required of an organization of the future. A graphic representation of this change might look like the illustration in Figure 6.2. Making this shift takes a good deal of time and effort, even among people who already consider themselves and their companies to be responsible. The difference is between social responsibility as an issue that concerns the communications or community relations or shareholder liaison departments, and social responsibility as a strategic issue that concerns the entire company.

Why introduce the idea of deriving a company's social responsibility from its stakeholder responsibilities? Because, first, the concept of stakeholders is one with which companies have made themselves familiar over the past few years; second, how companies define their stakeholders can make an enormous difference in how they implement their business idea (see the Celgene/thalidomide discussion in Chapter 3); and third, introducing the notion of responsibility to the stakeholder concept can help bring some rigor to analyses that oth-

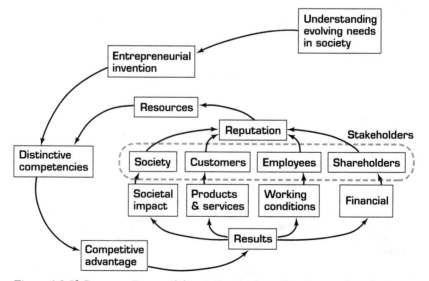

Figure 6.2 If Corporate Responsibility Is Perceived as Also Coming from the Business Idea Itself, a Company Can Increase Positive Results

erwise can become fuzzy. We have seen some stakeholder maps that include just about everyone on the planet—the consequence being that when you are responsible to everyone, you are responsible to no one. Al Dunlap, former CEO of Scott Paper, has stated: "The most ridiculous word you hear in boardrooms these days is 'stakeholders'. A stakeholder is anyone with a stake in a company's well-being. That includes its employees, suppliers, the communities in which it operates and so on. The current theory is that a chief executive has to take all these people into account in making decisions. Stakeholders! Whenever I hear that word, I ask: how much did they pay for their stake? Stakeholders don't pay for their stake. Shareholders do."

Dunlap's attitude is on one level deeply offensive—many thousands of Indians living around the Bhopal plant paid with their lives for their "stake" in Union Carbide. But to the extent that Dunlap is demanding more rigor in the discussion of stakeholder responsibility, raising the question of legitimacy is fair. Any company doing a serious stakeholder analysis should first identify those participants in its world who have the most direct interaction with its operations and should examine their interests from the participants' points of view, not the company's.

Before leaving this topic, we should note that people in business are not the only ones who bring assumptions to the discussion of social responsibility. To some social critics and NGOs, the problem is obvious: the system—capitalist, imperialist, global—is inherently bad, and so by definition, there is no such thing as a good company. We challenge this assumption as well, because we think a world that assumes good companies cannot exist will certainly not get as many of them as will a world that expects companies to behave well and puts pressure on them to do so. Even more fundamentally, we respect economic and commercial activity as a basic human impulse, one that ideally ought to bring not just sustenance but opportunities for creativity, personal development, and service to all of us.

There are also large numbers of people who, while not rejecting the market economy wholesale, feel that its current inequitable practice distorts corporate decision making so much that corporate expressions of change are often a cosmetic public relations exercise. A concise, contemporary expression of this point of view was received by our company, Global Business Network (GBN), from a long-term associate who no longer wanted to participate in our corporate strategy network. Actor, writer, and environmentalist Peter Coyote wrote: "the fundamental intention of GBN is to serve its corporate clients who to my analysis are directly responsible for many of the most egregious anti-democratic, exploitative, consumptive, polluting and homogenizing aspects of the New World Order...in the final analysis I do not want to serve my best ideas to Shell, Volvo, Exxon, etc. to help them 'green' their images with cute ads about kit foxes and seals while they exploit native peoples, desecrate the environment and obliterate national distinctions and currencies in the name of profits."

Peter Coyote's viewpoint is an important one because, first, it is shared by a significant number of people; corporations cannot ignore it. Second, his decision not to serve corporate ends is a moral choice that flows directly from his assumptions—as each of us, we hope, chooses to operate in a way that is congruent with our beliefs and values.

When corporations do behave responsibly, they can be important transmitters of knowledge and skills as well as sources of the societal wealth required to create jobs, entrepreneurial opportunities, and family security. A company could also have many internal reasons for developing social responsibility programs as a distinctive competency: to avoid public relations problems; to expand its risk management scanning; to experiment with new techniques in its planning process; to follow through on personal concerns of the board, the CEO, or other management; even to identify potential new business opportunities. Motivation is probably the least important aspect of the choice to undertake the task of reperception; results and new understandings are what count.

Steps in the Reperceiving Process

What kinds of activities contribute to the reperceiving process? Some actions have already been suggested. In this section, we summarize those suggestions and develop them further as a set of corporate next steps in the reperceiving process.

Think about the Issues

One of the first problems to address is that companies by and large spend no time thinking about these issues unless prompted by a crisis. Until then, these issues are "soft" issues, not hard ones deserving of management time. (Texaco CEO Peter Bijur said that whenever he had imagined a serious crisis hitting Texaco, it involved a disaster at a production site, an oil spill, or similar event; never once did he imagine a crisis around the issue of racism.) At a GBN meeting in The Hague in the fall of 1997, we participated in several small-group workshops examining various aspects of corporate social responsibility. The discussions were energetic, the participants enthusiastic and thoughtful, and almost all agreed that the learnings had been both useful and important. Then one of us asked a particular group, "How much time has senior management in your company spent in the past year discussing these questions?" The response was a set of startled looks—nobody could recall a single minute that had been spent on corporate social responsibility.

Most multinational companies have great attitudinal deterrents to asking such questions. These issues may be discussed as public relations or philanthropic issues, but not as business problems—certainly not as important as completing the dam/bridge/pipeline/chip design/acquisition. Yet, crisis issues are more often on the minds of employees than managers might think. The first step in reperceiving, then, is for managers to provide leadership by example and be willing to spend time on the questions themselves.

Reexamine the Business Idea

Once management makes the decision to spend time on these matters, it helps to look again at the business idea. Examining, or reexamining, the company's business idea can be the start of a process that enables management to identify not only the competencies it already has to work with but also undetected threats to the business idea. We demonstrated this reexamination as part of the Nike business plan in Chapter 4. Deep societal values may be contained within the logic of the business idea itself—so intimately connected with it that violation of those values would represent a major risk to the company.

For example, the value of sportsmanship is an intrinsic part of the Nike business idea—the antithesis of the value of winning at all costs. Nike wants to represent sports heroes who win because they are the best, not because they have the biggest sponsors, or take drugs, or cheat, or any of the other things people do when winning becomes the *only* thing. A communications company, for example, may value objectivity, or reporting without fear or favor, and makes that value an intrinsic part of its business idea. A communications business that violates that norm or fails to defend it when threatened threatens its own identity.

Examining the business idea in combination with a stakeholder analysis will illuminate ways in which stakeholders can affect the dynamic of company success. Any of these pressure points—consumers' ability to boycott, good employees' decisions to leave, shareholders' disinvestment choices, government's ability to constrain a company through taxation or regulation—can help a company identify areas in which its own self-interest justifies attention to social responsibility initiatives.

Identify the Major Concerns

A company that has identified an area of concern or risk (sourcing arrangements, choice of regions or businesses to invest in, employee working conditions) suddenly understands why this topic deserves management attention and what the potential consequences of inattention might be. The concept of social responsibility also provides a potential new approach to reducing risks with which the company is already familiar. For example, many industrial companies and their unions are locked into narrow, win-lose battles over working practices, wage levels, and benefits. It is hard to change the terms of these battles; many of the same communications problems that arise between corporations and NGOs also arise in industrial relations. Companies that look at industrial relations in the context of social responsibility, that is, as a form of partnership with unions or other employee organizations, may reduce the polarization and resentment that often lead to damaging strikes or workplace problems.

Identify the Stakeholders

A company needs to identify the stakeholders to whom it is most responsible and develop working relationships with them. The innovative example of Celgene and the TVA (see Chapter 3) is a good model here. Technically, the TVA had no stake in Celgene's plans to develop and market thalidomide, but morally and in societal terms, the victims were among the most important stakeholders of all. The company therefore educated itself about the TVA's positions, researched the organization's history and concerns, and developed a dialogue around those concerns.

Let's look at a hypothetical example. A company is considering setting up a joint venture with a government that has a seriously bad human rights record. From our point of view, management must confer with both local and international human rights NGOs. The company at least needs to understand better the scope of the problems that may be encountered, but it also should consider practical ways in which its presence might improve the situation. This process is long and difficult but worthwhile if it prevents worse difficulties or harm to human beings. Taking this step is also a key way of establishing credibility and goodwill within a relationship; nobody wants to meet an important adversary for the first time in the midst of a crisis.

Do More Homework

Once a company has a better understanding of the stakeholders who care most about the issues that have been identified as significant, it needs to investigate more facts. What questions might those stakeholders ask for which the company has no answers? For example, what is the average wage the contractors in Asia pay their employees? in the United States? What decisions has the local plant manager made about facility security?

Stretch Networks—Internal and External

Many organizations forget that the most powerful form of learning is experiential. Perhaps financial staff need to see for themselves how contract employees are paid and how contractors are audited, instead of just getting reports from country managers. Perhaps all the country managers who work in environments in which they face serious corruption should be given a chance to meet and discuss the issue from a common perspective. Perhaps managers should be encouraged to develop linkages with NGOs who focus on issues of concern to the company—environmentalists, antidiscrimination campaigners, human rights monitors—to open up the boundaries of consultation and learning.

Think in Scenarios

Companies who have taken some or all of the steps covered so far should have enough new information to feed into a scenario-thinking exercise, allowing them to draw out more rigorous explorations of long-term futures that might require changes in the way they manage their stakeholder responsibilities. Some companies have done this deep thinking in cooperation with stakeholders—government officials, NGOs, customers—and found it helpful to discuss their different perspectives on neutral ground (the future). GBN was recently involved in a large-scale scenario exercise involving every sector of Colombian society. Government officials, opposition leaders, guerilla fighters, executives, NGOs, educators, church representatives all participated (the guerilla leaders by phone!) in an exercise designed to create alternative scenarios for Colombia's future. The results were published in major Colombian newspapers in the summer of 1998 and triggered a national policy debate that was more open than had been previously possible.

A smaller example, which followed from the Royal Dutch/Shell case discussed earlier, was a one-day meeting sponsored by Shell Sweden in early 1998. The company invited members of Amnesty International's Swedish chapter as well as several representatives of government agencies and other companies to develop scenarios for "the future of human rights." The corporate and NGO representatives, who had not met before, were able to use the environment of the meeting to explore each others' assumptions and concerns as well as to work cooperatively to study a topic they all cared about.

Build New Competencies

By this stage, companies should see what distinctive new competencies will be required to deal with stakeholder concerns. Does the company already have them? Does the company have the structures it needs to develop them? Perhaps most significant, is the management both demonstrating and communicating to staff the importance of these competencies? This stage is where failures of leadership and communication often swamp good intentions; social or stakeholder responsibility is, of all corporate activity, the least likely to succeed if led from below. Whistle-blowers such as the quality control manager at A. H. Robins (see Chapter 3) are, unfortunately, more often ignored (or even fired) than listened to. Such actions create the opposite of the culture of dissent that is most needed.

We want to cite one well-known exception to this rule: the conduct of William LeMessurier, the chief structural engineer whose firm was responsible for designing the Citicorp Tower in New York.

The story of his discovery of a potentially disastrous design flaw in the tower, and the organizational response to it, became not only an extensive and fascinating story in the May 29, 1995, *New Yorker* magazine but earned LeMessurier his own Web site from Case Western University's Ethics Center for Engineering and Science.

LeMessurier's discovery (prompted by the telephone inquiry of a graduate student) was that a combination of innovative design strategies and contractor changes to the building's plan had left the 59-story building in midtown Manhattan extremely vulnerable to quartering winds in a hurricane. In other words, there was a chance that in such a storm, the building might collapse, killing thousands. Once Citicorp's top executives were informed, they moved quickly to involve the Red Cross, the National Weather Service, and the Mayor's Office of Emergency Management to put in place an evacuation plan in case a hurricane struck the city before the necessary repair work could be completed. The work lasted from August until mid-October, 1978, by which time the building was judged to be able to survive even a 700-year storm.

LeMessurier fully expected, when he broke the news to his client, that he would be professionally disgraced and financially ruined. In the end, Citibank agreed to accept the settlement that LeMessurier's insurance company offered ($2 million) and to find no fault with LeMessurier's firm. The insurance company, in turn, concluded that LeMessurier, rather than acting in an incompetent or devious manner, had acted "to prevent one of the worst insurance disasters of all time." His reputation was enhanced—and his liability premiums lowered.

Integrate the New Competencies

With few exceptions such as the Citicorp case, we found that researching cases for this book was often depressing. Spending day and night reading about corporate insensitivity or misconduct can leave a person vulnerable to despair about human nature—or more particularly, about human nature *in organizations*. Because we humans identify so strongly with organizations that we belong to, they have enormous power to shape our behavior, for good or ill. This cultural pressure is another factor of social responsibility.

We have all read about psychological experiments in which people who would never cause others pain or suffering of their own volition appear willing to do so when instructed to by authority fig-

ures. We have wondered how Germany's Nazi rulers were able to
persuade their people to collaborate with or at least seldom resist, the
murderous acts of that regime. We need to remind ourselves, in this
context, that according to German industrialist Felix Thyssen, the
conservative representatives of heavy industry in prewar Germany
were contributing to the Nazi Party at least 2 million marks annually. According to Alan Bullock, author of *Hitler*, this level of funding
came about because "the industrialists came to see in Hitler the man
who would defend their interests against the threat of Communism
and the claims of trade unions, giving a free hand to private enterprise and economic exploitation in the name of 'creative individual-
ism.' " In the world today, similar concerns are prompting businesses
to support political structures that act murderously toward their own
citizens. That support may be through direct financial contributions,
as in the case of Hitler's party, or in more indirect forms, but the
process of individuals rationalizing (or refusing to see the consequences) of their actions is much the same. Despite the formation of
the United Nations, despite the post–World War II signing of the
first Universal Declaration of Human Rights, and despite the collective resolution "never again," we have despaired over our continuing
inability to act effectively when faced with contemporary genocides
in Cambodia or in Central Africa or in the Balkans.

Questions of individual and collective moral responsibility remain very much unresolved in the market world, leaving many of us
to wonder how the corporations we work for can sometimes appear
to operate in ways that we hope we would never do as individuals.
None of us, were we sole proprietors of our own businesses, would
choose joint venture partners like Nigeria's Sani Abacha or Myanmar's SLORC. And yet world famous corporations hold their noses
and do so because that is where the resources are. Sometimes the
reasons for these decisions can be found in very direct conflicts between values. Shell, for example, felt an obligation to its thousands of
employees in Nigeria as well as a reluctance to abandon a business
that was still profitable, if increasingly problematic. Companies may
also feel they can outlast the problematic regimes, because they have
often been able to in the past. In the course of a 30-year project, a
company may find itself dealing with many different governments
within a single country. But more often, the decisions that draw
public anger on companies are made with no consideration of values

at all, and this aspect of the modern corporation causes the strongest public distrust and anger. Despite the best advertising efforts of the market economies, world public opinion does not (yet) accept that profitability is the highest value humanity can aspire to. So the purpose of the steps we have described here is, in the end, creation of a deeper and broader set of values for the corporation—values that will be communicated in its operations as well as in its advertising and that will steer the company in the right direction when things go wrong.

One of the greatest long-term benefits of this process of value development is likely to be in employee commitment. As unfortunate historical examples have shown, people have an enormous need to identify with organizations, even murderous ones. A company in which employees feel loyalty and trust for their employer and pride in their identification with the company is likely to experience more productivity, more innovation, less friction in the workplace. When bright young people begin saying "None of my friends want to go to work for Company Z any more"—which we have heard said about several of the companies whose cases are included in this book—it is a sign that long-term damage is already being done. A company that has embarked on a path of social responsibility needs to reflect the results in operational reality so that employees have the opportunity to contribute and begin living these new competencies.

Focusing its effort on initiatives that flow directly from corporate operations also helps a company address the legitimacy question; the company is not changing or making policy to be interventionist or imperialist but because its own business activities require the change.

Support the New Initiatives

Companies must support their initiatives with positive internal and external communications strategies that include independent verification procedures. The point of creating innovative, socially responsible practices within an organization is not to improve its image, it is to improve the lives of the people the organization touches and thereby achieve a good reputation supported by reality. It is therefore crucial for a company to know, as much as that knowledge is possible, whether the required results are being achieved. If they are, then they can be continued, developed, and used to create a positive feedback system that will generate additional innovations and improvements from company employees.

As we have noted, however, business does not enjoy much credibility these days in terms of social responsibility initiatives. Companies have direct self-interest in establishing independent verification processes to support external communications about new initiatives, because over time those processes will establish the type of reputation for transparency that grows into credibility.

Although we have been writing in this chapter about immediate next steps toward reperceiving, and then acting on, corporate social responsibility issues, we want to frame these activities within a long-term context, because the long term is the time frame within which an organization should consider issues of social responsibility. We don't mean long term in the sense that socially responsible practices are issues to "think about tomorrow," but in the sense that they are issues whose significance only becomes clear over a period of years. Developing a social conscience is not done overnight, nor can it be subcontracted out to Conscience Temps, Inc.

Along these lines, we want to include here a comment on the role of corporate boards by Ron Loeb, Mattel board member:

> "What all this means is that issues of social responsibility can no longer be relegated to staff functions such as corporate affairs or investor relations. Good strategic planning and good corporate governance are inextricably bound together. Therefore, it seems clear that today social issues must be part of every corporation's board, as well as its management, given the increasing impact that a socially responsible worldview is having on business success. Since long term corporate strategy should be among the uppermost concerns of corporate boards, they must consciously consider the company's role in society, the ways in which socially responsible business practices affect consumer loyalty and the effect of human-istic employment practices on productivity, job satisfaction and morale."

Using the cases that we presented in Chapter 3, let us now address some of the current front-burner issues around which this thinking and learning process of social responsibility might occur within a company.

Cheap Labor and Competition—
Race to the Bottom?

As manufacturing systems have globalized, more and more attention has been focused on the disparity in employment conditions between the industrialized world and developing countries. Consumers and trade unions in the richer nations, as exemplified in the Nike case, have raised issues of child and prison labor, below-subsistence wages, and unsafe labor practices in the poorer countries. It has become clear that public expectations of corporate practice in these areas are rising—and not only for protectionist reasons. In other words, the arguments are not about bringing the jobs home, they are about objections to exploitation. Companies, for their part, feel they have no choice but to globalize production. Their new competitors are no longer South Carolina firms, or Yorkshire ones, or Portuguese—they are Vietnamese, Mexican, Chinese. As a result, if companies do not manufacture in these countries as well, they will simply be replaced in the market.

In this climate, companies are discovering that observing the letter of the law is not enough. Countries in the developing world often have minimum wages set well below subsistence level—in large part, to attract foreign investment and compete with other equally desperate economies. Is it legitimate, or is it political interference, for corporations to urge countries to raise (or lower!) their statutory minimum wage levels? Is it any more legitimate for companies to counter criticism of themselves by stating that such interference in politics is not appropriate (especially when history is full of examples of companies that do interfere in politics when they feel it in their interest to do so)?

Instead of taking a direct interventionist approach, the U.S. Apparel Industry Program is attempting to develop codes of conduct and systems of monitoring that will allow companies to act together, independently of legislative action, to pull up wages and working conditions in these countries. It remains to be seen whether this approach will work in the face of intense economic pressures in both consumer and labor markets. No single company, except perhaps Levi Strauss, has been willing to move out ahead on these issues, and it is significant, in this context, that Levi Strauss is privately held and not under the same kind of shareholder pressure that most other companies face.

The concept of a living wage, a wage high enough to carry a family out of poverty (as opposed to a minimum wage) is beginning to emerge, and not only in the developing world (see Figure 6.3). Tim Smith of the Interfaith Center on Corporate Responsibility has called the living wage the most intractable issue facing international manufacturers. So far, conventional wisdom favors the assumption that efficiency requires the downsizing and outsourcing practices that David Korten calls "the race to the bottom." The market triumphalists, however, may need to open their windows and listen to the sounds coming up from the street, which may be the sounds of conventional wisdom changing. Stock prices and GDP growth may not always be the ultimate measure of progress, and progress itself may come to be defined in more complex and less measurable ways than the eager boosters of the early twentieth century defined it—as new technology, new markets, new riches, growing with no end in sight.

Jay Ogilvy has stated, "Where modernity can be characterized by its optimistic faith in progress, postmodernism is less confident about the direction of progress." And an exhausted Russian liberal, cam-

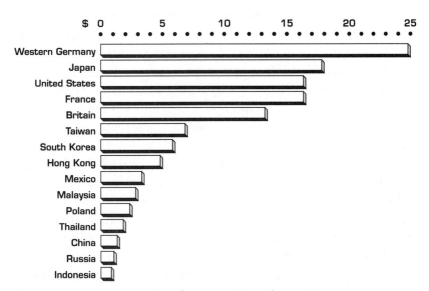

Figure 6.3 Labor Costs for Manufacturing, US$ per hour, 1994

Source: (© 1994, The Economist Newspaper Group, Inc. Reprinted with permission. Further reproduction prohibited. www.economist.com.) Published by *The Economist,* 2nd April, 1994.

paigning for the St. Petersburg city council on an economic reform platform, asked late one night in 1994: "Is this all you want of us? To be consumers? Is that all?"

This Russian democrat's question, from an outsider looking in, raises profound thoughts about ideology, not in a political sense but in terms of belief systems. For most affluent westerners, faith in consumption-led growth (which requires, in turn, low-cost production) is so axiomatic that we have long since stopped questioning it. We have organized our lives around consumption; estimates of the number of advertising messages each of us is exposed to each day range from ten thousand to one million (for New York City residents). Those advertisements may be on behalf of many thousands of products, but the underlying message, common to all of them, is that we must consume. We not only should have, but *need to have,* these sneakers, television sets, compact discs, and computer games in order to function in society. If we went to Pyongyang and saw thousands of images of Kim Il Sung, we would say that the citizens of that country were brainwashed. Is there any reason to think that our economic belief systems are immune from this unrelenting broadcasting, this chip in the brain that, Manchurian candidate–like, instructs America's teenagers to flock to the malls on Friday night? We westerners, who believe so unquestioningly in the rightness of consumption-led growth, have to start asking ourselves whether consumerism is in fact the highest value we can aspire to, whether its accomplishment is worth any sacrifice we might have to make.

Public concern over global manufacturing practices may represent the first signs of resistance to these assumptions. If the reality of globalization is that developing country resources are channeled into the manufacture of consumption goods for the affluent rather than into public goods such as education, health, and transportation systems, those workers may decide at some point that they would rather not be developed in this way. Another possible sign of resistance is the small but growing campaign by NGOs and poverty-stricken countries for debt relief, for cancellation of the existing burden of indebtedness to foreign banks that those countries now face. The campaign's argument is that the lives of human beings are being sacrificed to maintain the balance sheets of wealthy economies and that such a sacrifice is both unjustified and short-sighted in terms of world stability.

This issue also links up closely with increasing public concern over growing disparities in wealth and income, both within and among nations. After a recent study showed that Microsoft founder Bill Gates's personal wealth is equal to that of the poorest 40 percent of the population of the entire United States, consumer advocate Ralph Nader issued a challenge to Gates and other billionaires to find a way to address this problem seriously. (Gates has recently donated several billion dollars to his foundation, making it one of the largest in America.) This disparity is, to put it mildly, a key issue facing business and governments together, as two billion people enter the money economy over the next decades. Will those men, women, and children find productive work that enables them to integrate into their existing societies, or will they become a barely subsisting, angry army of the economically excluded?

What will the next economic movements, in fact, be demanding of international corporations? Will the movements be consumerist, in the sense that the 1960s revolution in the United States was co-opted into a set of lifestyle purchases, or will the movements be, in the historical American sense, populist? Is there an emerging populist consumer, a consumer who still wants to buy an expensive sport shoe, but prefers the one with a tag on it saying "This shoe was made by a worker who was paid double the minimum wage in his or her country"? Or is there an emerging army of the anticonsumers or the unemployed?

Environmentalism

Corporations have increasingly accepted responsibility for dealing with the environmental effects of their operations, especially in Europe. BMW is working toward a fully recyclable automobile, while Swedish paper companies are slowly eliminating bleaching and sulfites from their production processes. In the United States, corporate attitudes toward environmentalism have been slower to adapt (as one European executive asked us bemusedly: "What is it about American executives? They don't seem to care about the environment personally. You'd think they didn't have to breathe the same air or drink the same water everyone else does.") Even oil companies, hard hit by public reaction to oil spills like the Exxon Valdez, to damage to indigenous peoples' ecologies, and to the corrupt uses of petrodollars, have tried in recent years literally to clean up their acts, with varying degrees of success. Power generation facilities are developing more "green" sources of energy (wind, solar, hydroelectric) and in many cases are offering consumers a choice of source.

Where actual or potential environmental damage is more a side effect of a company's operations than inherent in the business, management appears to have less trouble accepting and paying for its environmental responsibilities. The centrality of environmental impacts is a good example of the distinction, for most companies, between Kees van Der Heijden's core business idea and the activities that surround it. Industries whose basic business has a direct environmental impact, however, like logging, have shown more corporate resistance and, as a result, have experienced the beginnings of more consumer pressure. In Europe, the use of tropical hardwoods is declining in favor of supposedly more sustainable North American supplies, and labeling programs for furniture manufacturers are becoming common. A major development in the industry, and a possible harbinger of bigger changes to come, was the announcement on June 13, 1998, that MacMillan Bloedel, Canada's largest lumber company, would cease clear-cut logging in the forests of western Canada. In his announcement, MacMillan CEO Tom Stephens stated, "Today marks the beginning of the end of clearcutting. It reflects what our customers are telling us...but equally importantly it reflects changing social values and new knowledge about forest ecology." This development took place even though the government of British Columbia had actually relaxed its environmental standards for logging—a fact that confirms the belief of Peter Melchett (Director of Greenpeace UK) that international political processes have shifted and that markets and businesses can often change much more quickly than politicians and governments can.

According to Melchett, environmentalists saw this shift most clearly in the aftermath of the Montreal protocol on the ozone layer. It became clear that the timetable of change with respect to chlorofluorocarbon emissions was not controlled by governments but by technology and business. When would alternatives be available? Who would manufacture, sell, and buy them? Greenpeace accordingly worked with London Polytechnic to develop an alternative refrigerator that was ultimately manufactured by an East German factory. The resulting technology (dubbed "Greenfreeze") is also lower tech and lower maintenance than existing systems and thus more easily taken up by manufacturers and consumers in developing economics. China's biggest refrigerator manufacturer has adopted the system, as have major producers in Europe. The lesson learned by Greenpeace and others was clear: Solutions are brought about by action, not policies, and that NGOs have to "recognise the limits of the political process and see companies as a major engine of change."

Companies trying to respond to their environmental responsibilities have more guidance—from their markets, as well as from legislation, regulation, international standards—than do companies trying to respond to other social concerns. This discrepancy is the result partially of the relatively longer history of standard-setting efforts and partially because many of the issues are susceptible to technical solutions, which are often easier for companies to take on than the soft problems. Environmental impact is also the area in which the legal trend exemplified in the Thor case described in Chapter 3 has been most clear: "Transnational corporations are increasingly being held accountable for their environmental performance in foreign countries... (including) the increasing occurrence of litigation in which a corporation is sued in its home jurisdiction on the basis of allegations of environmental harm arising out of the corporation's activities in a foreign jurisdiction."

Companies must move toward and demonstrate more investment in long-term solutions to the environmental impact of their operations. Cleaning up after oneself is of course necessary in the short term, but research into ways to reduce source pollution itself is the next-stage need, and demand, of the environmentally concerned public. As Harvard Business School Professor, Michael Porter, has argued, pollution is in itself a form of inefficiency in production, creating negative externalities that the market system has until now been able to displace onto the public sector.

According to Greenpeace's Melchett, "We live in a different world than when nuclear power was introduced." Consumers no longer assume that every technological advance is a positive one and no longer believe assurances that such advances are risk-free. Shell's Tom Delfgaauw made the same point when he described the move from a "trust me" world to a "show me" world, and an increasing number of markets seem to be agreeing.

Equal Employment/Racial and Gender Issues

Corporations generally encounter several kinds of operational problems in the area of racial and gender issues. One is the situation in which Texaco found itself—alleged noncompliance with equal opportunities legislation and the discovery that at least some senior managers within the company were not prepared to treat all their employees, especially their minority ones, in a nondiscriminatory way. Given that U.S. society as a whole contains so much racial tension, it is unsurprising that Texaco uncovered internal problems. The company did have a responsibility, nonetheless, to take a more active role in ensuring that its employees had access to equal opportunities within the organization and in protecting employees from being abused by employees with racist attitudes. After the crisis, senior management went further than insisting on compliance with the letter of the law; they built their internal Diversity Learning Experience around a positive statement about the value of diversity from a business as well as a personal point of view.

Shell provides another example of how diversity can work to advance other important corporate agendas. Its public campaign to try to persuade the white government in South Africa to enter into negotiations with the African National Congress was spearheaded largely by a senior executive who was both a minority and a woman. The campaign might still have taken place without her leadership, but Shell's original decision to bring her into an influential position clearly sent an important signal both to the rest of the company and to the government.

This approach expresses a broader understanding of the diversity issue: that corporate leadership has the potential not only to address internal problems of racism and sexism, but also to help improve the situation of minorities and women in the broader society. This commitment has been taken on board by other companies as well; Lotus, for example, has made antiracism the main theme of its philanthropic programs in the United States.

For most women, corporate America remains unconquered if not hostile territory. One of the few major corporations in the United States with a woman CEO, for example, is Mattel. Ron Loeb, a member of Mattel's board, has stated: "An example of how ethical, socially responsible and humanistic business practices may lead to better relationships between a company and all of its constituencies and, ultimately to more profit, is the removal of the glass ceiling in corporate America…Mattel's promotion of Jill Barad to the position of Chief Executive Officer is in conformity with a corporate culture which has consistently employed women in key positions and throughout the organisation in ratios well above most other major companies. I am convinced that this has made a profound difference in the attitudes and philosophy of the company." Most companies would still find it hard to take the steps required to make this kind of difference.

Some companies are focusing on women in management positions, but for most of the world's women workers, the problem is less the glass ceiling than the dirt floor. Despite rapidly increasing levels of female employment, women still account for barely 10 to 20 percent of managerial and administrative jobs in the world, and those positions are largely concentrated in marginal, low-paid sectors. The feminization of industrial jobs in export processing zones and other economic development areas (such as those taken advantage of by apparel manufacturers) has been highly beneficial to foreign investors, but less of a gain for those women who work for low wages, in difficult working conditions, and without job security. In Panama, for example, 90 percent of maquiladora employees are women. This phenomenon, which closely links to the labor standards issue described earlier in the discussion of cheap labor and competition, is being adopted as a major challenge to companies by the growing women's movement in the developing world.

Other related challenges for a company occur when its own employment values and commitments to its employees actively conflict with national customs or laws. This problem was faced by companies that, like Shell, chose to remain in South Africa during the apartheid era. Were the companies going to comply with the country's racist laws regarding employment, housing, and other benefits? According to the Sullivan Principles, which many of them adopted, the companies were expected to defy those laws, and many did. (One of us, who was on Shell's planning staff at the time, describes in the next section the actions that Shell South Africa chose to take.)

A similar but even more volatile situation is being faced by aid agencies and other organizations in Afghanistan, where the new Taliban regime has instituted prohibitions against women attending school, working, or even appearing outside their homes without a male relative. UNICEF Director Carol Bellamy has traveled to Kabul to meet with Afghan women about the situation and to try to persuade the authorities to change their policies. Women have been beaten, raped, and killed for violating the edicts, and organizations are confronted with a dire choice: defy the rules and risk the lives of their employees, accede to practices they would never tolerate in other countries, or refuse to operate in Afghanistan as long as these practices remain in place.

The Taliban experience highlights the fact that the integration—or not—of the world's women into the wealth-creating institutions of the future remains a huge open question. First, many traditional societies (as in the extreme example of the Taliban) do not believe that women should have access to economic activity in the ways that women in the industrialized world have become used to. This very profound difference in cultural viewpoints is already a source of conflict in many countries. Second, in subsistence-level economies, women may control important parts of their families' survival systems. Their level of control may decrease instead of increase as those families enter the money economy—a situation that will also not be sustainable in the long term. Although we do not discuss the economic and political role of women specifically in Chapter 8, "Issues of the Future," women's choices and aspirations are certain to have an enormous effect on the outcome of each issue we raise in this book.

When Bad Countries Happen

The Taliban example brings us to one of the most difficult issues of all: the problem of operating within an environment that is corrupt, murderous, repressive, or all of the above. Management may either unexpectedly find itself in such an environment (for example, after a coup) or decide, for business reasons, that they still need to invest and operate there. What should a corporation's response be to these situations? What are its responsibilities?

We believe that any company, no matter what it says, makes value judgments about where it will do business. No company will willingly remain in a country in which it cannot protect the lives of its employees. Whether the threat is an erupting volcano, a disease epidemic, a rampaging rebel army, or a government by death squad, the company will at some point leave, taking with it as many of its people as it can. The question is, short of such a dramatic situation, where does a company draw the line?

We propose that answers to this question should be sought first in the company's operations. Take the case of Myanmar, where forced labor and brutal relocations, especially of minorities, have been documented on government projects. It is an absolute minimum requirement, in our view, that a company that chooses to operate in Myanmar should avoid any use of forced labor in its own operations and should pay all employees a legal wage. But these steps are, for most of the public, too narrow a view of a company's responsibilities. The company can and should also refuse to allow itself to benefit from any forced labor involved in the project at all—in the construction of roads, the clearing of forest areas, the provision of supplies. If the company is going to protect its own employees from raids by saboteurs or rebel forces, it should also protect the communities it operates within from raids by government forces. If it is going to support those communities by building health clinics or schools, it should also help fund the legal defense organizations that protect community members from repressive judicial systems.

If the company wants to claim credit for doing such things, it will also need to commit to independent verification. Why should the public believe the company to be a force for good when there is no evidence to support the claim? The need for independent verification leads to the need to persuade such governments to permit organizations like the Red Cross, the United Nations High Commissioner for Human Rights, or Amnesty International to enter the country in the first place—a step that, again, the company should be prepared to take *on behalf of its own interests* as well as on ethical or moral grounds. If these actions cannot be taken, either because the government prevents them from happening or because the company is unwilling to take such positions, then the public can hardly be blamed for tarring the company with the same brush as its government partners.

The experience of Shell in South Africa during the apartheid era is a microcosm of the choices facing companies doing business in hostile environments. Almost every Shell employee in South Africa would have said, at the time, that apartheid was wrong and should be ended. The struggle to end it, however, posed a three-pronged dilemma for Shell involving moral, political, and business dimensions. Morally, the company felt it had a duty to work to end the system, especially since the scale of Shell's operations in South Africa meant that it could directly affect the realities and politics of the system. For example, Shell could—and did—integrate its housing at the Shell coal mines. The company could—and did—make available to black employees educational opportunities that in other companies were available only to whites. Company leadership could—and did—speak out publicly against apartheid.

Company executives believed that exercising active opposition while continuing to run a profitable business meant that they should not abandon South Africa. They were under great pressure to do so, because Shell was one of the last large companies to remain. Shell stations in Europe were being set afire by opponents even as Shell South Africa CEO John Wilson was being threatened with arrest by the South African government for speaking out aggressively against apartheid.

The anti-Shell campaign was extremely painful to Shell employees accused of being immoral profiteers. Inside the organization, one of the major worries was what would happen to local employees if the company left. The departure of other firms had transferred enormous amounts of wealth and assets into the hands of proapartheid white South Africans, with negative consequences for black employees in particular. Supporters of the boycott, on the other hand, argued that whatever good Shell might do by remaining was outweighed by the indirect support provided to the South African government and by the importance of international solidarity in the face of that government. They wanted Shell to stand with the rest of the world in making a pariah of South Africa.

These positions were hotly debated within Shell. Good arguments could be made for both points of view. One pointed exchange illustrating the complexity of the problem took place between L. C. "Lo" van Wachem (who, the chairmen of Shell's Committee of Managing Directors, had defended John Wilson from threats from the president of South Africa) and a group of Dutch church leaders. The clerics met with Van Wachem to inform him that their investment funds had decided to divest themselves of all Shell shares. Van Wachem pointed out to the clerics that, while he could understand their desire to express their moral position, he also was aware that they had profited financially from the share sale, and were they not concerned with the moral aspects of that profit?

This exchange illustrates the complexities faced by both executives and campaigners who are dealing with questions of investment and disinvestment. When business goes beyond purely economic tasks to engage more profound political and social issues, decisions do become more difficult. Looking back on this particular situation, most South African activists would say that the boycott did contribute to ending apartheid and that Shell got it wrong. Most Shell employees would still disagree, believing that they made a positive difference by staying. The answer, as in all such instances, is not simple.

Fundamental questions are raised when a company's host country experiences a change of government and its operating conditions change into something morally unacceptable. How does a company resolve its conflicting responsibilities (to its employees, its shareholders, its customers)? Even if the business numbers point to closing down operations, a company still has to deal with the negative impact on country employees, who will likely lose their jobs. The decision is made more difficult if disinvestment also means a negative financial impact or a foregone future opportunity. The complexity of such a situation cannot be overstated, but in the end, companies must remember that more than profits, or even jobs, are at stake.

Hostile environments provide another situation in which to use the scenario thinking we discussed in Chapter 4. For some companies, the response that "the people will be better off if we stay" is a knee-jerk, superficial response that needs to be backed up with rigor, not repeated like a corporate mantra. What might, indeed, happen if the company remains? What might happen if the company pulls out instead? These questions need to be answered realistically, as Shell South Africa apparently tried to do, and preferably in terms that even outsiders would find credible. What kind of economic impact does the company actually have on the country? On the government? Is opposition to an illegitimate government viable? Is it true that "someone else will come in," someone with a different moral view, and take the business, or is that situation unlikely? Will the government fall? Will other investors leave, or not? A company should construct at least two possible scenarios for its options and then ask itself: Under which scenario will fewer people suffer or die? A company may end up being wrong in its answer or in its decision, but at least it will have made its choice on a basis that its own employees—and most other human beings—can respect.

This context is an appropriate place to raise the issue of corruption, because this factor often weighs heavily in corporate decisions about investment and disinvestment. The issue of corruption also helps illustrate the distinction between a business ethics approach to corporate behavior and a socially responsible approach. There are many legal prohibitions against bribery and corruption—most notably the United States's Foreign Corrupt Practices Act—and almost all corporations have active programs to combat such practices. The emphasis in these programs is to prevent staff from taking, or making, illegal payments in the course of business operations.

From a perspective of social responsibility, corruption is bad not just for individual employees or officials but for the community in which the company is trying to operate. It decreases the legitimacy of social institutions and, by helping to create extremes of privilege and poverty, exacerbates social instability. Even if its own employees do not participate in corrupt transactions, a company that is simply associated with a corrupt regime is as much a target of popular anger as the regime itself. For these reasons, corporations are moving beyond an employee-centered approach to corruption. Unocal claims that, in an effort to ensure that revenue from the pipeline is not siphoned off by junta members, they have structured the government's share in such a way as to pay directly for new electric generating facilities in Yangon rather than to Myanmar's rulers.

Many NGOs are challenging the companies who continue to operate in partnership with repressive and/or corrupt regimes, like Unocal and Shell, to prove their good intentions by allowing independent verification of their claims to be making a positive difference. In Peru, Shell has taken the first steps in this direction through its contracts with indigenous NGOs to monitor the impact of its proposed natural gas project and community programs in Camisea. Shell has also stated that it will not operate behind a military shield. Unocal has so far chosen not to take either approach—indeed, independent verification would be impossible in Myanmar, because the government does not allow any such organizations to exist or foreign organizations to enter. When a company's partners are this recalcitrant and the company appears unable or unwilling to push for change, what lies ahead is a potential for continuing and increasingly violent conflict. Companies who believe that they can outlive such situations with their reputations intact have a difficult task: to convince a skeptical public that they are, on all possible levels, standing on principle as they practice their policy of engagement or run the risk of appearing simply cynical and self-serving.

Chukwudum Ikeazor, a Nigerian political analyst, police officer, and author living in London, has summarized many of the concerns presented in this chapter. The following statement is what he believes a multinational company needs to do to retain its credibility and reputation:

- Encourage government/opposition dialogue
- Enter into its own active and meaningful dialogue with the opposition, especially if its own activities are part of the dispute
- Enter into constructive and direct dialogue with local communities where the company operates
- Include community development as part of the company's operational costs and planning
- Include local community members in the company's workforce
- Never arm local security agencies or become involved with government security forces outside its area of operations
- Explicitly reserve the right to challenge or criticize government policies, even to the extent of ending operations and withdrawing, when those policies become so odious to the world or so harmful to the population that the company's own reputation suffers.

Ikeazor's last point raises the following question: On what basis does a company assert its values by criticizing governments? In the past, businesses generally asserted that setting values and norms was a job done by governments, churches, or other noncommercial agents of society. According to this model, business's job was just to obey the rules. The problem with this model is that, first of all, it was never true in practice. Governmental actions such as legislation, regulation, and executive orders lag reality—a situation arises first, the public reacts, and then government responds. Slavery is a good example. Businesses established the practice of slavery in the New World, and it took almost a century for the legal underpinnings of the system to be created (i.e., to remove all civil rights from Africans). It then took another two centuries for the system to be dismantled. Every piece of legislation affecting industry has been drafted and passed with industry participation in some way; the process has always been one of negotiation at best and outright vote-buying at worst.

The act of setting norms, then, has always been the result of complex interactions between key sectors of society, combined with other complex interactions among societies, and the entire set of interactions continuing to change over time. Today the system has been rendered even more complex by adding local, national, and international NGOs; media; intergovernmental organizations; and lobbying that is visible in real time on television, radio, or the Internet. Companies are participants in this process whether they like, or admit, it or not. Their responses to the operational issues they face are part and parcel of the system of setting norms every bit as much as a UN declaration, a British court decision, or an Oxfam position paper.

In this context, a company has every right to decide whether the net effect of its presence in a country is going to be beneficial or harmful to the citizens and to act accordingly no matter what campaigners might say. Even in a situation in which the company has weighed its options, made a difficult decision to engage with a repressive regime, and feels it has done the right thing, however, management may have to accept that the symbolic message to many of their consumers (or employees, or officials of a new government) will still be that the company is complicit in the harm done by that regime. These symbolic messages, translated as broad public assumptions (Royal Dutch/Shell supports the Nigerian dictators, for example, or Unocal supports the Myanmar junta), can often swamp any studies, analyses, protestations of neutrality, or advertising campaigns that the company may organize in its defense.

7

Business, Governments, and Non-governmental Organizations

More and more, companies are developing the understanding that the system of reperceiving social responsibility, described in the previous chapter, must evolve from backroom political horsetrading into more transparent forms of genuine partnership, a result of the new communications technologies and new public attitudes. Ironically, these pressures for change are arising in part from the very infrastructure that has been created to support the spread of markets through globalization. Thirty years ago, the concept of ecology as systems thinking was brand new to most people. The fact that the fate of a rain forest in Brazil might have an impact on European agriculture, or vice versa, was not an easy one for most traditionally educated westerners to assimilate. Today, with many millions of people hooked up to networks of one kind or another, these sorts of systems seem intuitively obvious. All sorts of rationalist dichotomies in our thinking are breaking down in the face of these experiences: mind versus body, science versus religion, national versus international, environment versus economy.

More people are realizing that human society grows and develops through the operations of complex interrelated systems rather than along millions of straight-line parallel tracks, but how does this realization affect the way business will interact with government and NGOs in the future? What kinds of changes will be involved, not only for business, but for the other parts of the system, such as NGOs and governments? What new institutions might emerge from these partnerships and interactions?

NGOs in the New World

It [the relationship with Celgene] is an uncomfortable comfortable relationship—trust but verify, and verify, and verify, and verify again.

—RANDY WARREN,
THALIDOMIDE VICTIMS ASSOCIATION

First, a disclaimer: The NGO community is too diverse and is growing much too fast to be neatly reviewed and summarized in a few pages. According to the *Yearbook of International Organizations,* the total number of internationally recognized NGOs is now well over 16,000, and the *Human Development Report, 1994,* estimates more than 50,000 local NGOs operating in the developing world. The Organization for Economic Cooperation and Development (OECD) estimates that $6 billion in development aid was allocated to NGOs in 1994. These figures show no signs of slowing down, which means that governments and corporations will face increasing numbers and increasing diversity of potential NGO partners and/or antagonists, ranging from those recognized by the United Nations, with millions of members, to those with a few dozen members in the rural countrysides and rain forests of the world. Their range of political views is also wide and covers every inch of the political spectrum.

Nonetheless, an NGO of any size or political orientation that wishes to be influential in the emerging systems of international economic decision making will have to think carefully about its role and programs. For years, NGO strategies focused primarily on changing national government policies; later, they expanded their focus to include intergovernmental organizations (IGOs) such as the United Nations, the Organization of American States, and the European Commission. Only recently have they begun paying increased attention to the general subject of business and social responsibility, putting their issues on the agenda of the Group of 8 (G8, the eight richest countries), Asia Pacific Economic Cooperation group (APEC), and other, more economically oriented international groupings.

The most obvious example of these changes in NGO strategy has been the environmental movement. Thirty years ago, environmental NGOs such as Greenpeace launched dramatic challenges to governmental and corporate practices that eventually resulted in the idea of sustainable development being mainstreamed into national laws and many corporate codes. The concept is far from being incorporated yet into the majority of business operations, but the attitudinal change since Greenpeace's founding has been enormous. Today even major international finance institutions (the International Monetary Fund [IMF] and World Bank in particular) are tightening their environmental criteria for major projects, and these institutions are encountering increasing challenges from NGOs in other sectors about their criteria for development and activities in general. (In fact, for the first time since their creation, the very reasons for the existence of these international finance institutions are being questioned.)

These economic and social issues are now at awareness trajectory points similar to where Greenpeace's issues were located in the 1970s. Global human rights organization Amnesty International (AI), as an example, has in the past focused its examination of business and human rights mainly on the issue of corporations supplying torture equipment or other items used to commit human rights violations. But in the last few years, broader issues of business and human rights have become important new topics on AI's long-term agenda. Its China campaign in 1996 was the first AI worldwide campaign to have as one of its central components a focus on the role of business, and corporations now feature in AI's reports on Colombia, Nigeria, India, and many other countries. Key AI national chapters are establishing business groups in which AI members (including those with a background in business) engage in dialogue with corporations based in their countries, and (as noted in the case of Shell Sweden in Chapter 6) businesses too are beginning to reach out to AI in order to improve their own awareness of the issues it monitors.

Similarly, corruption in the international business environment is no longer taken for granted. New NGO Transparency International has begin publishing country rankings for corrupt business practices, and governments as well as IGOs like the World Bank are taking those rankings seriously. The 1998 economic crisis in Southeast Asia has generated many op-ed pieces to the effect that corruption in its broadest sense contributed very directly to the collapse, because so much of the region's apparent prosperity was based on insider arrangements and investments that were unjustifiable on any grounds but personal aggrandizement. (*The Economist* of July 31, 1998, noted that the qualities that were praised during boom times—attachment to family, precedence of personal relationships over legality, and consensus decision making—were redesignated as nepotism, cronyism, and corruption when the crash came. Like in the Bofors case described in Chapter 3, western firms were often the beneficiaries as well as the victims of these practices.)

We agree with Monsanto's Toby Moffett when he states that new power relationships between NGOs and corporations are a "totally done deal." However, the fact that NGO-business dialogue about these difficult issues is increasing does not mean that it will be easy for either side to sort out a new way forward. The increasing number of public conferences, colloquia, and seminars on the subject of Business and Social Responsibility do not usually provide the sort of forum in which a corporate country manager can comfortably sit down and discuss with a human rights NGO how to deal in a responsible way with the *drogistas* trying to sabotage the company construction site or with the private security firm, recommended by the government, that turns out to be run by a former death squad paramilitary leader. Instead, organizations like Business and Social Responsibility are quietly hosting meetings for these types of discussions; in some instances, companies are going directly to NGOs to begin the dialogue.

Unfortunately, many companies find these kinds of initiatives still unthinkable. Even companies that are reaching out for dialogue, there are many executives who still do not believe that these initiatives offer any shareholder value. NGOs, in their turn, have been more comfortable demonstrating on the sidewalk than sitting in the marketing manager's office discussing minimum wage laws in Indonesia. NGO members may object to the very idea as a form of selling out and refuse to have contact with corporate representatives at all. Even if dialogue and problem-solving discussions take place, the fragmented nature of many NGOs may keep them from implementing their side of commitments. The deep suspicions of bad faith that remain on both sides may keep them from even meeting, let alone talking. However, the dynamics of the corporate-NGO relationship are changing despite each side's uneasiness. The baby milk boycott (see Chapter 3) provides an interesting example of this change. Initially, the NGOs formed around a situation in which the only way for them to achieve change in Nestlé's behavior seemed to be direct confrontation in the form of a consumer boycott. After four years, with the aid of intergovernmental organizations (WHO and UNICEF), an international industry standard was created. The NGOs then found themselves in the role of monitors and enforcers: Was the standard being observed? Where and how were violations occurring, and how were they documented? When would confrontation again become necessary, and who would make that decision?

As we observe the parallels between the NGO changes and the development of SA 8000 and earlier environmental battles, we conclude that what follows is the dynamic of the future. NGOs will play the following succession of roles as an issue develops:

1. An activist NGO floats an issue as a problem.
2. NGOs, usually in coalition, initiate a campaign to which public opinion responds either strongly (e.g., baby formula) or weakly (e.g. Disney).
3. With enough public response, governmental or intergovernmental bodies become involved, and NGOs participate in drafting new laws, regulations, or codes.
4. NGOs become active monitors of legal/regulatory/code compliance.
5. NGOs become resources to corporations in future policy decisions.

Bruce Williams of Celgene attributes much of the impetus behind the development of this pattern, at least in the health sector, to the AIDS crisis. AIDS patients, and those at risk of AIDS, were well organized and unwilling to be passively subjected to decisions made by the pharmaceutical or insurance industry. They demanded, and got, access to the tables at which the decisions were being discussed, and they set an example for other groups to follow.

From the corporate perspective, this sequence raises the major issue of accountability. Where does the accountability of an NGO come from? What earns them their place at the negotiating table? To corporations who are used to dealing with hierarchical structures and mainstream entities such as governments and who are used to justifying themselves in concrete terms to shareholders, NGOs may appear to have no legitimacy to even participate in discussions. (This belief translates into Chapter 6's final, most common assumption.)

An NGO may draw legitimacy from many sources. Some NGOs, like the Red Cross/Red Crescent, have behind them years of successful performance, long-standing relationships with governments, and enormous public credibility, demonstrated by the amount of financial support they receive from individual and corporate donors. Other, newer organizations may have won their legitimacy through public support as evidenced by donations and membership (e.g., Greenpeace, Oxfam, and Amnesty International, each with supporters and budgets in the millions). Some NGOs have achieved legitimacy through the quality of their research (e.g., Center for Science in the Public Interest or, again, Amnesty International). Finally, a key factor in NGO legitimacy, for business in particular, is the NGO's willingness—and ability—to negotiate and deliver an agreement that covers the issue on the table and not reverse course midstream or choose to play only to the gallery of its own supporters.

Corporations have been slower to recognize these sources of legitimacy than have governments, or even more crucially, the media. Governments recognize these organizations because they represent voters; the media recognize them because they represent information. And increasingly, it is information that matters most. Journalists cannot expect to be personally knowledgeable about the huge number of issues now of interest to the public, so an NGO that can provide news organizations with reliable and accurate information, *quickly,* is bound to become an important and trusted partner. Herein lies, however, the double-edged sword—for NGOs; as for companies, reputations built up can also be torn down. If information is the essential NGO product, today it is the media who have become the ultimate judges of product quality. NGOs had the advantage when they were competing only with governments to provide quality information; governments so often lied or failed to respond to issues or responded so slowly that NGOs were able to build up huge reserves of credibility by having their facts (mostly) straight and their responses timely.

The most important reason for the growth in NGO power is the loss of credibility of governments with respect to issues the public cares about. Peoples' attitudes may be well short of the radical antigovernment positions assumed by some U.S. organizations, but people still have a widespread sense that even though the government has a right to address an issue, it is unlikely to have the competence to do so in a productive way. Citizens who have interests that concern them deeply, such as child welfare, freedom of religion, or official corruption, increasingly look to the NGO community to speak and act for them. This shift has led to explosive growth in the number and membership of such organizations.

The balance of power has shifted somewhat since NGOs began taking on corporations. Corporations too have access to information and generally have much greater resources for distributing that information. NGO accusations can be challenged more professionally and more rapidly by a corporation than by a government. Thus NGOs now have more to lose in the marketplace of ideas if they gauge public opinion wrong or indulge in too much sensationalizing of the data. Greenpeace may have won the battle of the Brent Spar, but the organization also may have suffered from an image that its science was sloppy or distorted to fit its politics. The public has higher expectations of NGOs than it does of corporations and certainly of governments, so the risk of violating those expectations has greater consequences.

NGOs, then, will have to adjust to their new roles vis-à-vis business by taking themselves more seriously; by producing information that the rest of the world, not just their supporters, can trust; and by educating themselves about matters of which they might have little or no experience (the cost structure of international sport-shoe production, for example). These investments in themselves cost money, which is always at a premium in the nonprofit sector. A well-educated accountant capable of analyzing the financial filings of a multinational oil firm is not likely to work for NGO rates of pay, nor will an NGO's membership always think that hiring such a person is more important than hiring another campaigner for the Kenya office. Other skills that NGOs need to develop include negotiating and communication skills; they need to be as effective and build as much credibility in boardrooms and committee meetings as in public statements and press releases. Equally important, NGOs need to express their goals and mobilize to meet them, in terms of incremental achievements as well as universal demands, and to provide positive support to companies who help bring about those achievements.

Another great challenge to the NGO community, however, will be in rethinking its decision-making structures. Most international NGOs are much more democratic in their procedures than are corporations or, for that matter, many governments. This feature gives NGOs enormous strength in that they can harness the energy and commitment of many people, but it also may cause trouble and make them unreliable problem-solving partners. NGOs' unwieldy decision-making structures often inhibit them when they need to change their strategy or make quick decisions. Dealing with governments, which tend also to move incrementally and slowly in response to issues, was therefore not as difficult for most NGOs as dealing with corporations might prove to be. The NGO culture must preserve the power of its democratic base (and therefore its accountability) while it develops the ability to move, and act creatively, at speeds that will enable NGOs to be effective in the next century.

A second well-established feature of the NGO organizational culture is the NGOs' tendency to fragment, especially over ideology. The European Green Parties, with their Realos and Fundis, are a classic example, but the same splits often occur in other NGOs. As a result, negotiating partners may find that they are engaged in dialogue with an entire new set of spokespeople, or with a leadership that cannot speak for all its branches, or with multiorganization coalitions paralyzed by competing interests. As NGOs become more accustomed to operating on an international level, their own managements will have to adapt in order to address and overcome the difficulties that these cultural issues present.

Governments in the Globalized Economy

Development can no longer be regarded as the responsibility of government alone. It requires . . . partnership . . . with [the] private sector, labour and non-governmental organizations . . . There are many ways in which the special skills and know-how of the business community can help achieve development objectives.
—South African president Nelson Mandela

This statement is a far cry from the days, not so long ago, when populist politicians in the developing world could generally guarantee election by campaigning for expropriation and nationalization of foreign or private sector entities. Even as late as 1995–1997 in the United Kingdom, the defining ideological battle within the Labour Party (prior to its election victory) was over Clause IV, the plank in its platform calling for public ownership of the means of production. For years, the collapse of various forms of public ownership, from Russia to Peru, has shown that the public sector's share of national economies is shrinking everywhere. It has become a cliché to talk about the "decline of the nation-state." Globalization is taken as fact; facile comparisons are made between the annual turnover of corporations and the annual GDP of countries. National governments often seem not to be losing power but to be enthusiastically throwing it away in a race to deregulate, to divest, to downsize corporate-style, and thereby please the taxpayers. It has become government, as well as corporate, policy to let the market decide.

In this climate, it is no wonder that NGOs have emerged as ever more powerful forces. Peter Sutherland, formerly head of the GATT and now chair of Goldman Sachs International, has stated that the only organizations now capable of global thought and action—the ones who will conduct the most important dialogues of the twenty-first century—are the multinational corporations and NGOs. These two entities find themselves staring at each other across the table, not only because so many governments have left the room, but because their organizational as well as policy concerns truly are global: how to broker the desires of multicultural stakeholders, how to manage far-flung enterprises and operations responsibly and efficiently, how to respond to a changing international economy, and how to identify and communicate their missions in a swirl of competing values.

Many national governments, on the other hand, are finding it impossible to stretch beyond domestic political agendas to engage these issues in any real way. Take, for example, the United States's lobbying against the proposed International Criminal Court because of Congressional concern that U.S. soldiers might someday be accused of crimes against humanity. As a result, even supposedly global institutions like the United Nations or the IMF find themselves hostage to domestic political agendas, especially when it comes to their financial and budget activities. They are seldom in a position to take—or en force—genuinely internationalist positions on a given issue but must negotiate with individual governments in order to be effective.

To be fair, however, the nations are also finding it harder to act unilaterally, in practical terms—the growing question is, how does one nation regulate something like the Internet? By creating structures like the World Trade Organization (WTO) or regional trading blocs, nations try to control what they can and leave the rest to corporate decision making, since we now have chosen to live in the market world.

The emerging difficulty with these developments is that not everyone is well served by the market world. Although it is a matter of debate just *how many* are not well served and whether their numbers are growing or shrinking, it is impossible to argue that there is not a huge disparity today between the fortunes of the best off and the worst off. We have just concluded an 80-year-long experiment comparing two systems of wealth creation and concluded that the capitalist system actually does create wealth much more effectively; but the experiment has not yet established that the capitalist system distributes that wealth any better, or even well, in the long term. Whether a sufficient number of the world's families can survive, let alone subsist or thrive, in this world remains unknown. As long as millions of people feel that they have no stake in our system of wealth creation and that they can't survive within it, that structure will be at risk. Although on some levels, governments will still be sitting at the table reminding corporate managers of that risk, more likely NGOs will be calling the meeting instead.

The realignments of power are affecting supranational, or intergovernmental, organizations as well. The United Nations is launching a new study which will examine the relationship between the working methods and activities of transnational corporations and the enjoyment of human rights, and the director-general of the International Labor Organization (ILO) has announced that the ILO is launching a major worldwide drive to push for compliance with basic worker rights (including the prohibition of forced labor and child labor). The ILO points to several recent consumer boycotts as it notes that public opinion will attain increasing importance over the next few years. The ILO also notes that government and/or international sanctions will take a back seat to the sanction of the market. A growing number of multinational companies with subsidiaries in developing countries are searching for independent verification of their responsibility as employers and have asked the ILO to help them demonstrate that they are not exploiting workers and boosting profits by paying low wages. Intergovernmental organizations each have recognized NGOs with whom they deal and who increasingly provide them with necessary research, policy recommendations, and perhaps most important, credibility for the positions they might take.

As a result of this convergence of interests, most UN conferences today take place side by side with a doppelgänger conference, the NGO version. Even economic "summits" like the G8 meetings and APEC are beginning to attract similar encampments of NGO representatives, passing resolutions on the same issues, and submitting statements to the same media organizations. How long will it be before still newer institutions emerge—hybrids of NGOs and intergovernmental organizations? Hybrids of NGOs and business? What type of organization is an industry-created NGO that sets and monitors safety and pollution standards, like the International Council on Mining and the Environment? And how long will it be before these types of organizations break through the last barriers of national sovereignty, the way the IMF (for example) is increasingly accused of doing?

This last question is important because, despite everything else we have said in this chapter about the declining role of the nation-state, this notion is of little consolation to companies trying to operate in Nigeria, Myanmar, Saudi Arabia, or other countries in which the state not only maintains, but uses to the full, its monopoly on violence. There was no global appeal process for Ken Saro-Wiwa, none for Aung San Suu Kyi, and not even the benefit of posterity's regard for the thousands of citizens of those states who have been killed, tortured, or imprisoned without anyone to grieve but their families. These instances remind us every day that the nation-state in its most primitive form is still alive and well. If it were not, these victims would have had recourse to help from the international community.

New institutions are in the process of emerging in response to these needs, but the shape they will eventually take is still unclear, as is the extent to which intervention in the affairs of sovereign states will be tolerated by the international community. The business-government-NGO system of setting norms, then, has begun to look less like a tidy flowchart and more like a pot of soup being brought to a boil. Ingredients are added, begin to share flavors, and change shape as the heat of public opinion is turned up.

The Media—Turning Up the Heat

In 1993, when communist control structures were breaking down all across Russia, one of us was returning to Helsinki from a business trip in St. Petersburg and struck up a conversation with a Finnish lawyer on the plane. Aware of the long and difficult relationship—and geographical border—between Finland and Russia, I asked the lawyer if Finns were feeling any anxiety about military adventures by the unpredictable new regime. The lawyer replied, "Oh, we're not worried about the Russian army. We can handle them. What we're worried about is a bad winter and thousands of hungry Russian refugees showing up at our border accompanied by CNN." (Five years later, in the fall of 1998, the European Union as a whole was nervously making plans for such a possibility because of the worsening condition of the Russian economy.)

This anecdote reflects the fact that for all parties involved—business, government, and NGOs—the international media have begun to play a much more important role than in previous periods. When the heat is turned up on social responsibility issues, the international media now stoke the flames originally lit by NGOs. To most of the corporate world, journalists and NGOs share a predilection for scandal and bad news over coverage of positive developments or accomplishments. Good news about corporations is generally confined to the business segment of news broadcasts or the business section of the newspaper, whereas stories about scandals and exploitation make the front page. Once a corporate hero or villain has been identified journalists tend to interpret future actions according to that stereotype. For example, Shell (as part of its process of broadening the influences on its managers' planning process) invited a Tibetan lama to address participants at a management retreat. Rather than being praised for bringing in a different perspective, the company was blamed in some of the press for pursuing public relations goals instead of sticking to its business.

Credibility is a key factor in editorial decisions about the significance of corporate news. Many NGOs, at the moment, have more credibility with the public than do corporations or governments, so their critical reports or position papers are more likely to be taken seriously by media decision makers than are statements by corporate spokespeople, which often tend to be included in stories for balance rather than as the lead. The result is that news coverage of corporate behavior in society now reaches the public in a particular, usually unspoken context. Within that context are buried several assumptions, which might be summarized as follows: Business's only goal is to maximize profits; managers make decisions in terms of corporate self-interest and consider no other values; corporations have huge power but only choose to exercise it to dominate and exploit others, not to benefit society. We see this package of assumptions most clearly in popular entertainment media like movies, in which businessmen and women are usually the villains (as are, curiously, characters with British accents—so the most obvious movie villain, at least post–Cold War, is a businessman with a British accent!).

These stereotypes, however, exist side by side with other positive assumptions that the public makes about economics: that government should not intervene in business decisions; that entrepreneurship and independent, creative capitalism are good things; and that job creation (i.e., business growth) is the highest goal of economic development. This set of conflicting images of business helps explain, to a degree, the exceptions that the media makes. Virgin CEO Richard Branson, for example, has a positive media image because he *appears* to the public to be a human being rather than a corporate representative, whereas his competitor *appears* to be a businessman, with his anonymous, pin-striped style.

The most common media story lines involving business generally boil down to one of the following scenarios:

1. Unscrupulous, greedy businessman or corporation tries to exploit feisty workers or communities, who rebel and triumph over materialistic values. (See the movies *9 to 5, Norma Rae, China Syndrome,* and *Silkwood.*)
2. Communist or authoritarian dictator aims to take economic freedoms away from feisty *small* business sector and individual peasants/farmers/shopkeepers; democratic forces intervene and triumph. (See most war films from the 1940s and 1950s, and *Schindler's List.*)

The challenge to the media, and to individual journalists, in reporting on issues of business morality is to analyze the new developments on their own terms instead of as elements in old plots. As Mario Vargas Llosa states in his autobiography, "fiction makes its appearance everywhere, crops up in religion and science and in activities more obviously vaccinated against it. Politics, particularly in countries where ignorance and passions play an important role, is one of those fields that has been well fertilised so that what is fictitious, what is imaginary, will take root."

The same challenge applies to journalists reporting on business economics. Many NGOs assume that if a multinational corporation sponsors a particular initiative, that initiative will by definition harm workers or consumers. The standard business story line assumes that if an NGO makes a particular demand, implementation of that demand will harm employees or shareholders. The media needs to learn not to accept either perspective without doing a reality check. Child labor is a good example of an issue that is, in practice, much more complex than many of the stories about it. Responding to an earlier paper one of us wrote that discussed child labor by American firms' Asian contractors, a friend working for a development agency in Pakistan wrote angrily: "This is of course a particularly western point of view. What do they know about the options available to these children? If they are fired from their jobs with these companies their most likely alternative is the sex trade." Levi Strauss provides an example of an unusually sensitive corporate response: When the company discovered that its contractor in Dhaka, Bangladesh, was hiring 11-year-old girls as seamstresses, it negotiated an agreement for Levi Strauss to pay these girls wages while sending them to school. When they reach the age of 14, the minimum employment age set by the International Labor Organization, they will return to work.

The Levi Strauss illustration serves to remind us that while issues of morality can be very simple in principle, they can also be devilishly complex in implementation, and complexity is notoriously difficult for mass media organizations to deal with. It is imperative that the mass media learn and understand that anyone—corporations, governments, NGOs, even the media—can be wrong. What counts is finding human solutions to complex problems, a task that would become even harder without the careful involvement of responsible journalists. (Media coverage offers an interesting sidebar to the Citicorp Tower case presented in Chapter 6. Just as the *New York Times* began to make inquiries about the situation, the paper's staff went on strike. It is intriguing to speculate if, and how, events might have been different the incident had been subjected to widespread newspaper coverage at the time.)

Responsible journalism becomes even more complex when scientific evidence is involved and when public relations concerns or stereotypical story lines take precedence over the effort to determine fact. A good example is the cleanup of the Exxon Valdez spill. In an attempt to dispel their image of callousness and slowness to respond to the disaster, Exxon (and, to a certain extent, the government) ended up pursuing an aggressive cleanup program despite evidence from some scientists that the hot-water hosing of beaches and other practices were actually causing more damage to the ecosystem than the oil was. The great irony, in this situation, is that a company's need to overcome its evil media stereotype can lead to a worse, not a better, outcome on the ground.

Another great irony is that journalists are among those most at risk from abuse of power. Dozens of journalists every year are harassed, injured, or killed by the forces they criticize, while media corporations themselves remain largely silent. The defense of these broadcasters and reporters falls to advocacy organizations like PEN (which stands for playwrights, editors, essayists, and novelists), the Committee to Protect Journalists, and Amnesty International; the journalists do not rely on the resources and worldwide reach of media giants. Are these corporations neglecting important social responsibilities arising from their own operations, committing the same crimes of which they accuse other industries?

If a new partnership among business leaders, NGOs, and governments is to emerge around social responsibility issues, then, it will have to include development of new forms of relationship and engagement with the media as well, but not from the standpoint of image-making, spin, or the traditional public relations exercises that have given business communications such a bad name in the past. The watchwords of these new relationships will be transparency, credibility, and realism in the service of real improvements in the lives of real people.

One interesting aspect of the changes now going on in NGOs, governments, and the media is the possibility of new institutions emerging from the process. Current events in Russia reflect, to some extent, the problems created when financial and commercial practitioners try to operate in an environment that has no effective institutional infrastructure to support them. This situation is starting to appear globally. Are the IMF and the World Bank appropriate institutions to set the parameters for solving social responsibility problems? Is the United Nations? What would a hybrid governmental/nongovernmental organization look and act like? The phrase itself shows how dated our existing terminology has become. The debate, during the Uruguay Round, over international labor standards in the context of trade agreements; the campaigning of trade unions around NAFTA; the campaigning of international NGOs around the OECD's proposed Multilateral Agreement on Investment (MAI)—all these political negotiations demonstrate new forms of decision making in formation and reflect the search for a new balance. As one Canadian activist has stated about the MAI: "singling out trade and investment independently of justice and health and sustainability and governance simply no longer has resonance with democratic populations. A deep feeling of unease arises from attempts to impose agreements like the MAI without imbedding them in related agreements. A concern for shareholder equity needs to be replaced by a concern for stakeholder equity." These sentiments could be applied to any number of issues we have raised in this book and point effectively to those issues we can expect to pass on to our children to deal with in turn.

8

Issues
of the Future

*The final artwork can be seen as a simple
metaphor, of society as a room that we are all in
together; a society built on the remnants of an
industrial past and whose equilibrium and future
direction is determined by the way in which we
decide to walk together.*
—Max Couper, *The Plot,* 1998

The future is arriving sooner and sooner every day. The scenarios
that GBN prepared in 1997 for the future of Japan were overtaken
by events before they were even printed; many of the cases in this
book will require serious updating, we are sure, by the time it is published. Innovations, insights, and increasing consensus around key aspects of corporate social responsibility will be appearing in our
newspapers increasingly in the coming years.

We can expect more innovation in the area of social responsibility not only because new relationships are emerging among the major players, but also because new problems are emerging for those
players to deal with, problems that will shake up existing assumptions
about our world and will require a good deal of cooperation and
skill to resolve. Our historical review in Chapter 2 might have suggested that there is "nothing new under the sun" with respect to social responsibility of business, but in fact, there is. Technologies are
being explored today that raise more complex issues of scientific responsibility, perhaps, than corporate decision makers have ever faced
before.

One of the most discussed of these complex issues is cloning, the
creation of new living creatures from cell tissue rather than from old-

fashioned sexual reproduction. Ever since the birth in 1996 of Dolly, the sheep who was the first clone to attract global attention, politicians, scientists, and the general public have been weighing in with opinions on the ethics of this scientific breakthrough. As Gina Kolata states in her book *Clone,* the first time the Group of Eight nations at an economic summit ever voted on an ethical issue, it was to oppose human cloning. And yet, the positive potential of cloning, particularly in terms of medical applications such as infertility treatments or using cells from patients with cancer to create bone marrow and other organs needed for transplants, may ultimately overwhelm the initial public fear.

The cloning issue, for all its sensational press, is a subset of the broader technological debate over genetic engineering, the intentional changing of life's basic structures. Because of these innovations, the impacts of which are not yet clear, the biotechnology revolution may become the defining issue of the next century in the way that the discovery of atomic energy shaped the consciousness of the entire postwar world in this century. Will we someday see the biotech version of J. Robert Oppenheimer waging a war against a product or an industry of his own creation?

In a 1997 lecture presented to a UNESCO Congress in Kobe, Japan, bioethicist Glenn McGee suggested that the next 100 years would see "changes more dramatic than the twentieth century, which saw the creation of molecular genetics, the rise and fall of eugenics and the human genome project." According to McGee, there are three waves of coming change in the field of genetic engineering, and there are institutional weaknesses that may require reform if our societies are to deal with these changes.

The first wave is new reproductive technologies and the conflict between parental and fetal rights. If parental rights are taken as primary, as currently exists in the United States and Europe, both infertile and fertile parents are allowed to do as they like in terms of genetic testing and embryo diagnosis. If fetal rights are taken as primary, then the parents have a concrete responsibility to act in the fetus's best interests even before birth. The highly politicized nature of this debate is exemplified in the recent controversy in the Netherlands over a couple's decision to abort a fetus that was determined to have a defect leading to blindness. Organizations for the blind criticized the potential parents strongly for acting as if, in their view, blindness were a condition justifying the "killing" of a child. Should parents have the right, once they have the diagnostic capability, to have only perfect children? What are the responsibilities of testing services and laboratories in this context?

The second wave is how genetic testing might be used for public health purposes. As McGee points out, eugenics quite rightly turned public opinion against societal plans for master races and other forms of genetic manipulation, such as the sterilization in the 1920s and 1930s of more than 20,000 persons in the United States, 45,000 in the United Kingdom and 250,000 in Germany. Nonetheless, in the long term, insurers and health agencies are likely to want to develop guidelines for passing on potentially lethal genes. Is state-sponsored genetic counseling for couples the first step back toward eugenics? What if the public sector does not involve itself so that only families who can pay are in a position to take advantage of testing and counseling? Are the families with money being provided with an unconscionable advantage? How should health care facilities, testing labs, and product manufacturers respond? Should they be involved in policy choices on these issues, given their commercial interests?

Finally, McGee points to "maldistribution of public resources in health care" as the third major ethical issue. Billions are spent on genetic research by both the public and private sectors while basic public health initiatives go unfunded. If the biotech industry keeps its eyes on the prize of commercial return, will simpler, less remunerative technologies with more immediate potential to aid humanity go undeveloped?

At the moment, no institutions are clearly responsible for holding the required conversations, setting the boundaries, and making the required choices about these questions. In the current climate, decisions will end up being made by the market and, in cases of conflict, by the courts. In which direction public opinion will move in response is hard to predict, especially since our opinions about these issues are inevitably affected by the fear caused by disclosures about the unintended effects of other technological innovations. The public is increasingly aware that technologies we have already put in place might have started time bombs ticking in our bodies. For example, two teams of researchers, in the United States and in Denmark, are now asking whether the pattern of declining male proportion of births is linked to a similar pattern of increasing birth defects of the penis and testicles, increasing testicular cancer, and declining quality and quantity of sperm. Both groups of scientists are hypothesizing that all these patterns are linked to exposures to hormone-disrupting chemicals, including dioxin, pesticides, lead, solvents, and smoke stack emissions from smelters, steel foundries, and incinerators. And both groups are hypothesizing that the relevant exposures are most likely taking place before birth, in the mother's womb.

These hypotheses are lending support to campaigners' fear of other potential forms of unanticipated damage to our personal and collective ecosystems. As we saw in the Greenpeace/Brent Spar example described in Chapter 3, the root of most campaigners' objections to these new biotechnologies is simple but profound, and their arguments are not, at bottom, about technical issues. Their objections flow from a conviction that biological systems are more complex than scientists can understand and that therefore our experiments are a form of hubris that will end up causing some great unanticipated harm: "Don't mess with nature."

Biotechnology companies, on the other hand, insist that their innovations will help reduce, rather than increase, such problems by aiding diagnosis, identifying potential biological hazards, and providing individuals with more control over their reproductive lives. Companies also claim that their research can help prevent future damage by decreasing the agricultural sector's reliance on pesticides, since food crops can be genetically engineered to be resistant to insects such as the corn borer, and that these new strains represent real opportunities to reduce world hunger by increasing yields in poor countries. According to Toby Moffett, vice president of international government affairs for Monsanto, the decision about genetically modified food products is a "feed the world" issue, not a technological issue.

With these arguments in mind, the U.S. Department of Agriculture has supported the use of genetically engineered (GE) crops, approving them as safe enough not to require labeling, segregating from other crops, or any of the other initiatives demanded by critics. In keeping with the U.S. government's history of heavily promoting U.S. agricultural products overseas, the introduction of Monsanto's genetically engineered soybeans into Europe therefore featured what Monsanto's Moffett described as "typically clumsy American tactics," which were perceived by European governments and consumers as a heavy-handed combination of governmental and corporate power. Like other companies discussed in this text, Monsanto discovered that its broad stakeholder conversations should have taken place before, not after, its public relations battle began.

The genetically modified organism (GMO) battle has been especially heated in Europe, where the European Commission in September 1997 adopted regulations requiring labeling of food produced from genetically altered soybeans or corn (maize). Greenpeace has campaigned hard against Monsanto's products, stating that "if the food multinationals have their way, millions of tons of engineered crops will be grown." For Greenpeace's Peter Melchett, the key question for his organization's anti-GMO food products campaign is, "Can we stop the release into the environment of GE [genetically engineered] material through market mechanisms?" From this perspective, if the market demands GE-free food products, then alternatives will dominate despite the best efforts of Monsanto, Novartis, and the U.S. trade establishment. (Melchett feels the future of chemical agriculture generally is to be replaced by a new organic paradigm.) Monsanto's perspective, on the other hand, is that the existence of a GMO-free niche market is fine, as long as there is a balanced assessment of the positive potential of biotechnology products in the food industry.

Greenpeace's campaign illustrates the size of the stakes, for it is true that these innovations have the potential not only to change entire industries but to affect every consumer's life very directly. A person can decide not to buy Nike sneakers, not to drive a gasoline-powered car, or not to have genetic testing before conceiving a child, but once genetically altered soybeans enter the food production system, it will be, in all practical terms, impossible not to eat them.

The question of bioethics could be one of the hardest questions faced by our emerging norm-setting systems. Unlike spiritual knowledge, technological knowledge is cumulative; future generations cannot forget how to split the atom or splice genes. If we decide, for moral reasons, that we do not want to use certain technologies, the decision must be made consciously and must be enforced. As we have seen with land mines and biological and chemical weapons, making and enforcing such decisions is not at all easy. And even fewer international organizations are equipped to deal with these bioethical questions than to deal with arms control.

For any given technological innovation, three facts hold true: (1) Its inventors can never completely foresee its eventual impact; (2) some element of the population will welcome it, and (3) some other element of the population will object to it. What a perfect recipe for uncertainty. Twenty years from now, will we be praising the gene splicers for inventing the crops that produced the first famine-free decade in human history? Or will we be prosecuting them for negligence on a global scale as we shovel genetically engineered soybeans into empty missile silos, to rot safe distances away from our supermarkets?

Another issue for the future is the potential for responsibility-related crises among the clean technology companies. So far, the main public opinion concerns have been around traditional business issues such as competitive policy (Microsoft), which have not involved aspersions of grave harm to individuals. Manufacturers of the software components included in weapons systems, for example, have not been as targeted by campaigners as hardware manufacturers have. Will this apparent immunity change in the future, thereby exposing these companies as well to the risk of public opinion crises?

Other, nontechnological, issues may shape the future of business and social responsibility. Changes may occur, for example, in the public's definition of risk and therefore what public opinion considers a crisis. As Paul Shrivastava points out, the Three Mile Island nuclear reactor near-meltdown in 1979 was clearly a crisis, one that caused enormous social disruption and changed the face of the American nuclear power industry. Yet not one person was killed in the incident. In contrast, the 50,000 deaths that occur annually in car accidents are not perceived by society as a crisis because of the social structure surrounding automobiles—and also because of people's greater willingness to accept hazards that they expose themselves to voluntarily. The public's acceptance of this level of risk could change and cause a change in attitude toward the automobile industry.

Similarly, larger questions around the nature of work—and worklessness—are becoming public hot buttons. The General Motors strike in the summer of 1998 involved thousands of Americans directly in questions of downsizing, outsourcing, and the responsibility of corporations to the communities they create and sustain. From the company's point of view, the critical issue of the strike was the right to make strategic decisions about cost-effectiveness—to outsource and to adopt new technologies (for example, plastics instead of steel). From the union's perspective, the critical issue was about jobs disappearing around them, the future disappearing from their children and communities, and their inability to fight that process directly. The danger to both sides, of course, is that a death spiral sets in and both parties go down in each others' arms, which is what some observers think happened to the U.S. steel industry.

In America, these issues are being fought out within a legal environment that is increasingly hostile to unions. In the opinion of one attorney who is an expert in industrial relations, employees in the United States now have little or no effective right to organize. Companies can fire organizers or union advocates and have to pay, at most, nominal fines after long court procedures during which the plaintiff employees have had to find jobs elsewhere. This climate poses particular challenges to union leadership in industries in which unions do have power. What are the trade-offs between jobs—of any kind, at any salary—and security? Do unions have responsibilities only to their members, or also to their surrounding communities and to the larger, unorganized workforce?

In addition, the structure of work in future organizations may be attacked as socially damaging in an economy in which knowledge is the new capital. The assembly-line manufacturing paradigm of the late nineteenth and early twentieth century, for example, which was organized to produce the greatest number of lowest skilled and monotonous jobs, tends to drive down education levels in the surrounding community. Low education levels in turn keep workers out of new and growing fields of work. These factors have led to increased calls for business to assume greater responsibility for education—blurring, again, the traditional line between government and the private sector and blurring as well the traditional oppositional relationship between economic efficiency and social welfare.

Related strong linkages between social responsibility and corporate governance will also emerge during the coming decades. For many employees, the most important aspect of their company's character is the way they themselves are treated—whether their treatment comports with their sense of fairness. This traditional attitude is compounded today by new demands and expectations on the part of knowledge workers, who want more participation, more creativity, and less hierarchy in their work lives. Will those workers reject existing definitions of status and success? Will the growing disparities between worker and executive compensation become an even more volatile issue? (In 1991 the highest-paid director of British Airways earned less than 11 times the company's average wage of $17,000; in 1996, only five years later, that director earned *50 times* the average wage.) Will shareholders and other stakeholders begin demanding that boards more closely oversee corporate decision making in this area? Will new generations of workers be satisfied with the current structure of corporations and their essentially undemocratic concentrations of power? Under what circumstances might we see a resurgence of union activism or new models of labor advocacy? Will employees, two generations from now, be electing their CEOs?

Different cultures have different views on these questions. Until recently, European societies and the Japanese have valued high-stability, low-incentive employment policies as a route to social stability, while American and developing economies have pursued policies that result in much thinner safety nets for workers and their families. Much of this debate is actually over the economics of burden sharing: Should corporations, through high-employment policies, contribute to the maintenance of the safety net, or is the problem purely a public (read: taxpayer-funded) problem? Companies (e.g., General Motors) and indeed whole countries (France) are facing national strikes and disruption over these deep issues of finding a balance between industrial efficiency and workers' needs. Trade unions in the United States and elsewhere are confronting enormous challenges as they struggle to redefine their own strategies and goals in the context of this battle.

The question of balance at the heart of many of the present and future dilemmas described in this book is turning up in public consciousness in more and more ways.

One of the most publicized discussions of balance is the notion of the Third Way that has been proposed in the United States by the Clinton administration and in the United Kingdom by the centrist Labor government of Tony Blair. In political and economic terms, this concept refers to finding a balance between the laissez-faire model of economic activity exemplified in the United States and the social welfare model exemplified by postwar European governments. We do not intend to offer an analysis of the Third Way concept in this book—we leave such an analysis for far more expert political and economic commentators. We believe however, that the emergence of the Third Way as a theme in public debates over governance flows directly from the public's concern about the principles by which an economy ought to be governed, and that concern flows directly from the new debate about corporate power.

An illustration of the heightened levels of concern about the need for such a balance was brought to our attention by an unexpected source. British artist Max Couper created a massive installation on the subject of balance in a German museum in 1997: an actual Thames River barge poised on the fulcrum of a huge steel traiangle, the entire edifice kept in balance by two giant steel springs as people moved around inside it (a literal representation of pushback). The artist, who intended among other purposes to illustrate that even a multiton object could be moved by individual humans if balanced right, showed us how he had understood the project to be an illustration of the balance between culture, government, and business (see Figure 8.1), taken from *The Plot*, the October 1998 book about Couper's exhibition).

A final issue for the future will be the extent to which the concerns presented in this chapter filter down from the most highly publicized cases, involving the largest and most visible companies, into the rest of the business world. Campaigners and activists often have more information about large companies and have a powerful lever with which to move them: the attention of the international media. What about the smaller but much more numerous firms whose behavior attracts less notice? What mechanisms will encour-

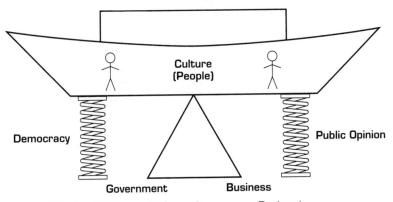

Figure 8.1 The Steel Fulcrum (Culture, Government, Business)

age them to ask themselves the same questions we have proposed here, or what enforcement strategies will prevent them from pursuing dangerous operational practices below the public's radar? Clearly, industry leaders need to respond to these issues.

In an effort to think creatively about what may lie ahead, we have sketched out, in the next chapter, some brief scenarios for how corporate social responsibility might operate in several possible worlds.

9 | New Stories

In late 1997, GBN began working on new global scenarios to describe four possible futures that could develop over the next 20 years. The scenario team built these four futures around seven kinds of driving forces: globalization, technology, climate change, organizational structures, geopolitics, and world population trends. From their work emerged very different visions of how the next century might begin. The current versions of these four scenarios are summarized in this chapter along with accounts of how business might deal with social responsibility—or not—as each future unfolds.

1. In this scenario, a series of crises cripples global comity, leading to an increase in the number and power of identity-driven ideologues and leaving the disaffected on the periphery. The climate problem is bigger, more complex, and more dangerous than anyone predicted, and it comes on the heels of worldwide financial instability. Current technology is insufficient to make the difference, and world leaders repeatedly fail at the critical moment. Small-scale violence mounts as regional populations compete for newly threatened resources and nations direct their frustration toward their neighbors.

Between 1999 and 2012, the world saw more social chaos across the globe than since the 1920s and 1930s. An arrogant generation of leaders, who had known nothing but unbridled prosperity in the last decades of the twentieth century, did not expect prosperity to ever end and were not prepared to lead their nations through the crisis when it did.

The crisis began with the mismanagement of the Year 2000 problem, the computer network breakdown that wasn't supposed to happen. Financial records and transactions began to reveal bizarre errors. The worst impact was in Europe, where the collapse of the European Community's information systems hit at the same time as the attempted implementation of European Monetary

Union (EMU). The United Kingdom, which had opted out of EMU, ended up pulling out of the European Union itself to save its economy.

By the end of the year 2000, what statistics were available indicated a massive shrinkage of world economic activity. The sector known in Germany as the Mittelstand, the great band of jobs-producing midsize corporations, was the hardest hit; most multinationals had enough reserves and redundant systems to survive, and small firms had never been as dependent on computer networks to begin with. Unemployment soared across the developed world; some states and provinces in the United States and Europe had to reduce their school years by half as tax collections plummeted. Birthrates dropped to levels never before experienced as couples took advantage of new contraceptive and genetic testing technologies to ensure that they would not have to support children, especially disabled or unhealthy ones.

In this terrifying economic environment, corporations that were left standing faced enormous demands on their resources. Strapped governments, unable to provide adequate public safety services, demanded not only that businesses establish their own fire and police forces but that those forces act as backups to those of the public sector jurisdictions in which they operated. Companies around the world eliminated their philanthropic programs and poured any available cash into meeting essential needs of their immediate communities; the socially responsible ones did, at least, and earned a degree of gratitude from their neighbors that they had never before enjoyed as people moved into company-constructed housing, attended company-supported schools, and ate in company cafeterias. The companies that refused to help withdrew within guarded walls and became targets of angry and violent attacks by vigilante groups.

These new initiatives carried over from the industrialized economies into the developing world. How could Ford justify putting $1 million annually into the Detroit public school system and ignoring the struggles of similar systems around its Indian factories? Such corporate social responsibility was expected because everyone suspected (without proper accounting systems, it was hard to tell) that despite their economic troubles, multinational corporations were actually not in bad shape. Mass unemployment had depressed wages to levels below those of the 1970s, largely compensating firms for the collapse of many of their markets. Trade unions almost vanished—workers wanted jobs, at almost any salary. Instead, the new forms of collective bargaining were between community leaders and facility managers over what services the company would provide to surrounding areas.

Environmental activists, on the other hand, became more and more aggressive as the extent of climate change became clear in 2008. Waging a last-ditch stand against the oncoming "whiplash cooling" that was expected to send glaciers cascading down across Northern Europe, northern Asia, and Canada by 2090, small bands of guerilla fighters targeted manufacturing plants in particular in attempts to ratchet industrial production down even further. Split off from their traditional NGO allies, who were more concerned with protecting jobs and forming alliances with the companies who provided the main financial stability in their communities, the environmentalists grew more marginalized and violent. Never mind that their campaign could not make up for the lack of will that environmental "protection" agencies and agreements had shown in the twentieth century and that it came too late to stop the catastrophe— the Greenwarriors were going to go down fighting.

In this climate of institutional failure and looking out for oneself, the Greenwarriors were not the only paramilitaries around. Human rights NGOs in anarchic states reluctantly began taking up arms to protect their communities from the depredations of unpaid military units and criminal gangs, forging uneasy alliances with the weapons manufacturers they had once campaigned against. For both parties, it was preferable to see these relatively principled organizations asserting control and maintaining order than to allow the downward spiral of collapsing states to continue.

By 2012, with the United Nations in a shambles and international financial organizations closing down, a group of international business leaders realized that if they did not act to restore some confidence in the global economy, no one else would. The Declaration of Corporate Responsibilities was signed by 100 CEOs of the world's largest companies—American, Chinese, Japanese, European, and South African. The declaration pledged that these corporations would use their financial and economic power to stabilize local economies wherever they operated. Highlights of the declaration included that the signatories would:

- Hold the line on jobs, only reducing workforces when operating losses reached a designated level
- Contribute at least 1 percent of their aftertax profits to local government entities to support crucial public safety and educational services
- Commit 50 percent of their research and development budgets for the next 10 years to efforts to mitigate the effects of climate change
- Most controversially, refuse to pay corporate taxes to governments that had assumed power by violent means

The declaration received huge public support, and other companies found themselves subjected to intense pressure to adopt its principles. As corporate commitments to the declaration spread, only the Greenwarriors and certain fundamentalist groups objected to the blurring of lines between corporate and government responsibility. Such groups believed that these powerful elites had created the twenty-first century's enormous problems in the first place, and the declaration did nothing to reduce their guilt. Because of the threat of violence by their former allies, other, more mainstream NGOs remained silent concerning the declaration, supporting its signers locally but not daring to take public positions in favor.

As economic and political stability slowly began returning to areas covered by the declaration, the majority of the public was grateful that somebody—anybody—had finally taken effective action.

2. This world evolves slowly, but successfully, out of the status quo. The pragmatists are in control. Complex problems such as climate change and international crime resist quick solutions but nonetheless yield to incremental progress and cooperative attention. None results in a serious crisis, and economic growth maintains a low and steady rate. In a largely peaceful world, negotiation and compromise secure gradual social improvement as inequality erodes and communitarian, middle-class values take hold.

By the second decade of the twenty-first century, the developed world was beginning to relax and enjoy the end of the volatility that had characterized the previous century. A few glitches around the Year 2000 problem had occurred, but they mostly provided joke material for late-night comics, nothing more serious. Generation X had profited by the example of their irresponsible and self-indulgent

Boomer parents and grew up vowing to be good stewards of the resources they inherited. Their values were much studied and analyzed: They believed in strict honesty and transparency in their business dealings, swift and severe punishment of criminal activity, traditional family life (but in many nontraditional family configurations), personal development rather than conspicuous consumption in their spending habits, and caution rather than aggressiveness in either social or economic innovation. As one social commentator noted, they were like "the Amish with cars."

As a result, a wave of self-regulatory initiatives swept the international business community after the turn of the century. International agreements in which national minimum wage laws were superseded by living wage criteria were negotiated by companies in the apparel, agricultural, and retail sectors. CEOs of many of the newly successful technology companies signed pledges to keep their compensation to predetermined multiples of their companies' lowest paid workers. Almost every one of the new international standards was midwifed by the powerful mega-NGO EarthRight, formed in 2005 by a merger between Greenpeace and Amnesty International. EarthRight, with offices in 150 countries and industry specialists covering 40 sectors, also claimed responsibility for the 2010 agreement in which 80 countries agreed to install trial monitoring video equipment in all major courtrooms so that the International Commission of Jurists could evaluate whether defendants were receiving fair trials and whether there was reasonable doubt as to a judge's impartiality or competence.

Helped along by the shocking evidence of the first courtroom monitoring experiments, more and more developed countries passed their own versions of the U.S. anticorruption legislation. Many companies simply refused to operate any longer within countries in which bribery and kleptocracy were rife and pulled back into more mainstream markets. Companies that chose to remain in high-crime countries began making demands that governments take stronger steps against criminal and corrupt elements and backed those demands up with funding for judicial reform programs. A measure of the impact of these initiatives was that even the Russian government, by 2010, was able to prepare and implement a massive campaign against its biggest criminal gangs, effectively breaking the power they had held for 20 years. It was also a measure of the change in political climate that even human rights and civil liberties groups failed to complain about such campaigns.

On the other hand, the world's steady economic growth led to an equally steady shrinkage of national safety nets. A new consensus emerged (even in France) that health and education were the only true entitlements that the public sector owed its citizens; the rest, even retirement arrangements, were up to individuals to provide. New reproductive technologies were subsidized by the state, and potential parents were reminded regularly of the goal of creating a generation of "only healthy children." A huge new financial sector emerged, providing low-cost and conservative but reliable savings mechanisms for low- and middle-income households. There was a minimum of regulation, but new laws provided for harsh criminal penalties for white-collar crime, with the result that financial scandals like the one in the late twentieth century became a rarity.

The major threat to this hard-won stability was climate change, but the new political leadership of the developed world was able to take advantage of the shift in public opinion to put in place measures that greatly reduced the danger. Late-twentieth-century American politicians could have never anticipated the 200 percent increase in gasoline taxes that passed the U.S. Congress in 2004. The revenues helped fund and therefore accelerate the switch to hybrid-electric vehicles in the developed countries. The timing of this shift helped offset the enormous number of new gasoline-powered automobiles on the roads of developing countries.

Another potential threat to stability, the mass movements of economic refugees, never materialized. In many developing countries, the steady growth of small and medium-sized businesses meant that low-wage workers could find work at home instead of having to emigrate. With the numbers of immigrants declining, the antiforeigner political parties of the late-twentieth century were deserted by the public. The public in turn demonstrated that they were willing to let into their countries just about all who wanted to enter—provided, of course, that the immigrants were financially self-sufficient and led quiet, assimilated lives. Immigrants who found themselves unemployed or in trouble with the law could expect to be immediately deported—despite the protests of civil liberties organizations.

While corporate philanthropy remained an important aspect of business operations (eventually coming to fund almost 75 percent of total theater and museum budgets in North American and Europe), the main public demands on corporations, throughout this period, were not for cash contributions but for transparency and equity in their own operations. Companies were expected to compete fairly and to spread advancement opportunities and benefits as equally as possible among all employees. For some companies, this responsibility extended into their neighboring communities; a consortium of financial firms, for example, established an international educational foundation whose mission was both to improve local schools and to provide the top 20 percent of students in those schools with guaranteed entry-level positions in the funding companies. "It's in our own interest," the chairman of the consortium stated pragmatically as he announced the opening of the foundation's Peruvian office.

3. This future is one of perpetual transition, driven by elites who use technology to solve every problem—including those that technology itself creates. Immediate challenges are resolved more swiftly and painlessly than anyone expects, while the barreling global economy produces unprecedented prosperity and modernization. At the same time, rapid technological change forces correspondingly deep and sometimes disorienting social change.

Around the year 2000, the world's information technologists entered a period of creative ferment. The Year 2000 nonproblem had unintentionally accelerated the pace of change by concentrating the minds of all the major systems developers on a single issue, one that forced them to focus on developing, over a very short time frame, the first truly cooperative networks that shared key standards and communications capabilities. Once the technologists succeeded, they realized that they were in the best position yet to respond to a more positive challenge: to build an information system that could contain the explosion of scientific knowledge and could coordinate, at last, all the systems. The result was the Adaptive Analysis Engine, which became the core logic of the Problem Solving System (PSS). PSS proved to be the moment when computing finally graduated into human affairs, and by 2012, its extension into human disputes was happening everywhere.

PSS first proved its worth in detecting potentially dangerous mutations in gene therapy experiments, providing a fail-safe shutdown procedure for pharmaceutical company research labs. New generations of PSS then proved to be equally effective at screening out problematic mutations in bioagriculture—a development that resulted in an out-of-court settlement of the 20-year-old class action suit against a consortium of chemical companies, thus clearing the way for public acceptance of genetically engineered food. These developments were typical of the early applications of PSS: Technology solving problems that technology itself had created.

The first use of PSS in human dispute resolution came in resolving the long-running consumer boycott of manufactured clothing. The Home-Sew movement, building on the Gandhi revival and on the widespread availability of home CAD/CAM and other newly cheap design software, had persuaded millions of consumers in the developed world to stop buying manufactured clothing, since it was impossible to be sure that the clothing had not been produced in exploitive conditions. Movement organizers were finally persuaded by ASEAN's manufacturing lobby to try letting a huge PSS application tackle the issue by reviewing all available data on production costs, wage levels, and wholesale and retail pricing in 235 countries and on international labor standards and factory inspection reports. The result, six months later, was a report identifying 14,506 standard-compliant factories in 57 countries and recommending appropriate wage levels sufficient to support a family with the demographics of the typical worker in each individual factory. The Home-Sew board agreed to call off its boycott on the condition that a PSS-generated monitoring program be put in place at each of the sites where apparel production was taking place. (By that time, however, enough consumers had come to actually enjoy making their own clothes that a whole new high-tech cottage industry had grown up around the boycott, and a large part of it survived to become the next generation of popular designers.)

Despite such apparent triumphs, however, not everyone was happy with this world of digital, deracinated elites. The widespread availability of safe and cheap forms of contraception and the global communications networks that gave women everywhere information about them were direct challenges to many traditional societies, as was the widespread use of genetic testing (considered "playing God" by religious leaders). The ability of women to work surreptitiously from home at computers supposedly purchased strictly for entertainment turned out to be a massive form of civil disobedience in countries in which it was illegal for women to work. Electronic delivery systems for primary education became more widely and cheaply available, leading to more highly educated populations demanding more accountability, and more employment, from their governments.

Some governments tried for years to control the new networks, but the flow of information was unstoppable. Even imprisoning people for violating the antitechnology laws proved to be more and more difficult, because activists equipped themselves with transmitter implants and their homes with tiny camera monitors as protection against surprise inspections or arrests.

Individual creativity in using technology for empowerment finally won out over the state's power to use it for surveillance and control. Some people felt threatened by the ultimate homogenization of world culture and the loss of treasured, historic traditions, but the capacity of the new systems to archive and preserve those traditions, if only digitally, provided some consolation.

The new businesses that emerged and thrived in this environment faced one very complex question: If the value of their networks depended largely on the number of nodes, or users, they could scarcely afford to write off whole countries or regions where potential users could not afford their products. Companies also were not happy about being criticized as "elitist" and "Euro-American info-imperialists." The costs of wiring the developing world (with or without wires) was clearly going to be enormous, however, and governments were not prepared to pick up the tab.

In the end, it was a MicroNet initiative that set in motion the beginning of a solution. To celebrate the 10th anniversary of the company's founding and the launch of its new palm-sized communicator-computer, the MicroNet CEO announced that the company was simply going to give away 50 million of the devices in developing countries, along with the code for replicating the device's core functions into older technology such as digital television sets and radios. Agreement had already been reached with the Teledesic network to provide the required capacity to bring all these new users on-line. Even governments who found the offer horrifying were forced by the enthusiasm of their citizens to assent.

One of the great benefits of these developments was economic transparency of a type no one could have imagined 30 years earlier.

At the urging of social activists, the technology corporations joined together to set up community-based library-type facilities where volunteer programmers could spend time at company expense writing applications for solving all sorts of human problems, large and small—land disputes, boundary arguments, liability issues. In the hands of NGOs, a PSS using these custom applications could scan food distribution systems and spot hoarders, whether public or private, and bottlenecks; in the hands of consumer activists, the PSS could scan retail networks and spot gougers. Banking secrecy laws were a thing of the distant past as soon as special PSS programs began monitoring offshore transactions, a development that led to the sudden voluntary resignation of several dictators. This future is truly the world of which Esther Dyson, the publisher of Release 1.0, spoke decades ago, in 1998, when she told her listeners that technology would ultimately mean "the end of the official story."

4. This world is the dark side of perpetual transition: a world in which rapid technological growth, geopolitical tension, and inequality combine to produce widespread social dislocation. Advanced technology, society, politics, and economics gradually all fall under the control of a rootless international elite, who push their powers to unethical extremes. There is an increasingly violent response from fundamentalists. Both Europe and America gradually wall themselves off from an outside world that is growing increasingly lawless, decadent, and inequitable. Populist social unrest is rampant in both industrialized and developing regions.

By 2001, thanks to the efforts of the skilled programmers who had helped avoid the Year 2000 crisis, the speed and reach of networks had created the perfect liberal economy that had long been predicted by optimists in the West. Its guiding principle was freedom for business, freedom to trade information, hire and fire and change locations at will, and avoid any significant form of government regulation. Executives could even rent cyberaddresses that would enable them to evade all forms of personal taxation. By 2005, this practice was not even considered illegal in most countries; it was regarded as just another of the privileges that set the elite off from the rest of humanity. (As a businesswoman of the previous century, Leona Helmsley, had presciently observed, "Only the little people pay taxes.")

The business community, unfortunately, did not handle its new freedoms well. Rather than distributing the new beneficial technologies widely, the most successful firms colluded to control supply and prices as tightly as they could. With the margins they were earning, they didn't feel they needed to enter new, high-cost, low-return markets. In addition, the uncontrolled spread of organ farms and baby factories, established by the biotechnology industry to cater to wealthy citizens' desire to extend their life spans and overcome the epidemic of chemical infertility, caused deep anger and resentment in the poor countries whose populations provided much of the raw genetic material for these products.

These developments fed antitechnology nationalism in many of the struggling countries of the world, who reacted by withdrawing, as best they could, from systems housed in the United States and Europe. Only their young people stayed wired—computer centers became the twenty-first-century equivalent of the slightly dangerous-looking coffeehouses of eastern Europe under Russian rule, with defiant young men and women wearing their Levi jeans and downloading their American rap records.

The international, cosmopolitan elite gradually walled itself away in urban enclaves—the countryside was just too dangerous in most of the world; low-grade terrorism spread with each new conspiracy theory on the Net. The corporate rich were blamed for mysterious new diseases, for food shortages, for the disappearances of activist leaders. The gulf between rich and poor widened to a chasm that almost nobody tried to cross any more except the Ecumenical Prophetic Church (EPC), formed from a 2008 merger of the Reform Jewish, mainstream Christian, and Sunni Moslem faiths. The EPC, with its 200 million members, agitated continually for what it called "economic and social justice for the excluded"—but nobody seemed to be listening. As the CEO of MicroNet stated in 2010, when asked by CNN reporters for his opinion of the latest EPC manifesto: "Those people are excluded for a reason—we don't need them."

Not only were those people not needed, they were turning into a problem. Splinter groups from the EPC, frustrated with their movement's failure to achieve reform, joined with more fundamentalist sects and began sophisticated programs of bomb attacks on manufacturing facilities and cargo ships. A crucial blow against civil society took place in 2015 at a Mexico City summit called by the EPC and the remaining major international NGOs (Greenpeace, the Red Cross/Red Crescent, Oxfam, and Amnesty International). A huge bomb exploded during the conference's final plenary session, eliminating the leadership of all the participating organizations at a stroke. The EPC blamed American-supported corporate mercenaries; the Mexican-American Governing Council blamed "leftist fringe groups." No serious investigation of the attack ever took place.

What few civil liberties remained in most countries fell away as the decimated NGOs tried to regroup. The wealthy sector of the populations (both government and corporate officials, along with the more respectable criminal element) demanded, and got, harsher and harsher penalties for antisocial behavior. The era reminded some historians of the previous century's Golden Eighties, when one of the early elites (American banker Felix Rohatyn) had predicted the arrival of an era of "private splendour and public squalor." In that more innocent time, he had meant the comment as a criticism; but now it was a proud statement of fact.

10 | Getting Personal

Despite globalization, business people are
prisoners of their culture and don't realize it.
—PETER MELCHETT, GREENPEACE

The scenario sketches in the previous chapter are not meant as road maps. If anything, they are meant to prompt questions, perhaps along the lines of the question we sometimes ask ourselves when reading or hearing about someone faced with a terrible challenge: "What would I have done in a situation like that?"

If we were senior executives living in each of the four futures, what would we have had to decide each day? How might our decisions have changed the story? What actions, taken now, would help us make whatever decisions we each might be facing in 5 years, 10 years, 20 years? And for that matter, what actions could you take now to prepare you for dealing with your own version of the cases we summarized in Chapter 3: your Nigeria, your Bhopal, your boycott, or your Dalkon Shield?

We hope you will use this context in considering the next several pages, which may strike you at first as out of place in a business book. In Chapter 6 we listed several "next steps" that corporations could take in reperceiving this question of social responsibility, steps that could lead to new understandings and potential shifts in strategic direction. But we as individuals also have a need to check our own assumptions and to act according to our own sense of responsibility. The "next steps" that follow, then, are personal—not corporate—ones.

Stop and Think

Before taking any action within your company or organization with regard to the issues we have raised in this book, take the time to think first about the source of your own moral convictions. This step is a very personal first step because you, the person reading this, have your own life history, capabilities, and concerns. Even if you have worked for the same company for 40 years, this book is addressed to you as an individual. Who are the people you listen to with respect—your heros? Many of us have someone we unconsciously check with in our minds when faced with a problem—a parent, grandparent, teacher, religious leader, or public figure. What values does that person or figure represent to you? Wherever your own beliefs about right and wrong come from—a family member, religious faith, humanist belief, pragmatic desire to get along peaceably in the world, or a combination of all of these—this source is your starting point for the rest of the chapter.

If, as we expect you might, you find it problematic to consider bringing your personal moral convictions to bear on your work, we propose a few considerations. First, the belief that work is a totally rational and impersonal activity, as opposed to family or community life, is hard to sustain in reality; this belief is one of those rationalist dichotomies that is giving way to holistic or systems thinking. If we are honest with ourselves, we can readily admit how our emotions are tied up with our work lives, how we treat our work as a form of community. Beyond this basic fact, seeing company managers in the midst of a crisis—as we each have—is to understand even more clearly the personal hurt felt by every employee. Staff at Union Carbide, in the weeks after Bhopal, spoke of watching colleagues crying at their desks. Using employees' moral concerns and emotional energy to help prevent such crises is much preferred over the task of cleaning up the damage afterward.

Second, most of us, even without such crises at work, have had at least one moment in our lives that has shaken us profoundly out of our daily habits of mind. It might have been a death or a close brush with death; it might have involved us directly or one of our loved ones. If you have had such an experience, as we have, we are sure that one of your reactions was the same as ours: a sense of changed perspective and a vow never to let inconsequential things loom so large in our lives again. These vows, unfortunately, seldom survive the onslaught of dailiness that follows after the crisis passes. Our sense of what is truly important becomes buried under layers of denial and routine. This first step of self-examination is just another way to remind ourselves of what we truly value and to keep it alive in our minds.

Understand that we are not suggesting that, if you volunteer on weekends at a homeless shelter, you have an obligation to open a homeless shelter in your corporate headquarters. We proposed in Chapter 3 when we discussed specific cases that social responsibilities are best understood in terms of direct operational issues. If a company facility is located in an area with many homeless people, doing something about that particular problem may be justified. If not, surely the company can find other ways to express the same concerns.

Our third consideration is an anecdote: In the 1960s and early 1970s, we were both active in the anti–Vietnam War movement. At one student meeting at Rensselaer Polytechnic Institute, some members of the audience argued: "We can't get involved in political issues here—we're only here for nine months of the year." The question that followed logically was: And if you're only home the other 3 months of the year, does that mean you are excused from involvement a full 12 months of the year?

What we are suggesting is that our lives are comprised of whole systems, not separate compartments. If we cannot be fully ourselves at work (which is where we spend most of our time and energy during our lives), where can we be? And what values will we, in our turn, represent in our children's memories when they stop to think about their own heros?

Identify Your Opportunities

Do some research to identify opportunities within your reach to act on your convictions. Our previous step was such a personal one because, simply, the process of determining the best way for a business to be socially responsible is every bit as complex as determining how to be a moral person in a difficult world. You will be more likely to be able to help your company solve its problems of responsibility if you have been as thoughtful as possible about the issue on a personal level.

This step requires some research. What are the challenges facing your own business or the industry it operates within? What sorts of conduct are businesses in your industry criticized for? What worries keep you and your colleagues awake at night? Which of these issues falls within your particular function? Answers to these questions should help focus your inquiry. If you are already deluged with information on these subjects (if, for example, you are the EEO officer for your firm), try to identify the most important questions you feel the company faces and ask: Is the company really doing everything it should about this issue? (Remember the Texaco Scenario: Policies are not enough.) Are there questions management is evading or answers management is refusing to hear? Where is denial strongest within the organization? Are there ways you can contribute to internal conversations—formally or informally—to help create a positive atmosphere in which to move these issues forward?

Join Your Colleagues

Try to identify colleagues who may have common interests and join forces with them. One of the major reasons for corporate concern about social responsibility issues is the bad publicity that companies like Shell, Nike, Nestlé and others have faced. For many managers, the unspoken worry is, "there but for the grace of God . . ." Others in your company may share the same values and anxieties and would like to explore ways to bring the company into line with those values as a preventive measure before, not after, problems happen. If you are a CEO, can you talk to other CEOs who have valuable experiences to share? If you are a senior manager, do you have colleagues in other countries who have grappled with the same problems you have? Do you have access to an employee union, organization, or club where these issues can be raised? Can you start one?

These suggestions themselves lead to another significant question: Is there a culture in the organization that encourages this type of exploration? The existence of an open atmosphere, a culture of debate and dissent, is crucial to successful learning and problem solving, but such a culture is much more the exception than the rule and needs to be constantly supported to survive. "Group-think" is a congenital disease that every human organization begins developing the day it is born; management's job is to determine whether it develops into full-blown mental paralysis. A macho culture that dismisses all social concerns as soft and not suitable for real management attention can also discourage 360-degree thinking.

The employees of the future, or at least the best ones, will be less likely to tolerate a stifling, top-down work environment. Better educated, better networked, these employees will demand more participation in decision making or they will leave. They will also, we feel, demand more congruence between their own moral values and their employer's. Remember the phrase from Chapter 6: "None of my friends want to work for Company Z any more"; it may be an early indicator of long-term trouble. Many people we have discussed this book with told us that they had left at least one job because they were being asked to do things they thought were wrong. Even in Japan, it is not at all clear that the contemporary version of the Chisso chemist would keep his findings quiet.

Seek Out Epiphanies

This step may sound quite melodramatic, but it harks back to the type of experience we described earlier in this chapter, the one that changes a person's entire perspective on life (at least for a little while). These events generally happen *to* us and often in a negative way. Someone who has seen a loved one die, for example, can turn into a lifelong crusader against cancer, handgun violence, drunk driving, whatever the source of pain and death was. We don't often find positive ways to *make* these changes in consciousness, or direction, happen—and we should. Some people do it through a volunteer project, perhaps with a community group or NGO; some do it through travel. The important point here is that the most powerful learning is experiential, and most managers, by a certain point in their careers, have stopped having unpredictable experiences. Their lives are simply too ordered and too determined by their corporate identities—as Peter Melchett of Greenpeace put it, "company people move around the world in a company cocoon." (For some CEOs, just the experience of being with people who neither know nor care what their name or position is would be disconcerting enough, let alone being with those people in a refugee camp, African schoolhouse, or rain forest village.) These experiences take effort to arrange, but when they are implemented with thought and care, they can be invaluable.

An example of a CEO seeking out experiential insight was reported in the *Sports Business Daily* on April 29, 1998. At the height of the anti-Nike campaign, CEO Phil Knight appeared unexpectedly at a University of North Carolina–Chapel Hill course on "Economics, Ethics, and Impacts of the Global Economy." That day, three student groups were presenting their analysis, with recommendations, of the Nike labor practices case. According to the university newspaper, Knight sat in the corner of the room listening to the students' recommendations and later spoke to the class in response, describing Nike as a "changing company that had already instituted reforms." Knight certainly did not have to attend this class personally, but in doing so, he was seeking out an ephiphany.

Use Your Learnings

Use your learnings to test changes in the organization. This personal step links up with the corporate reperceiving process we outlined in Chapter 6. If more members of Congress, for example, forced themselves to go out and look firsthand at the situations they legislate about (without benefit of staff, handlers or interested parties), they *might* pass less ineffective or harmful legislation. Under normal circumstances, legislators simply do not learn anything that helps them understand what the unintended consequences and real impacts of their proposals will be. People who run companies cannot afford to understand as little as politicians do about their businesses and can initiate experiments on their own to test their assumptions.

With the learnings acquired from following the first few steps presented in this chapter, an individual employee or manager can begin thinking about ways to improve practices and about implementing a genuine reperceiving process. A board member can begin thinking about the types of information being provided to the board. Are management information systems feeding back, at all levels, the basic data needed to understand the system? Do you have, for example, independent information about the wages being paid in your Asian contractors' factories, or are you relying on their assurances of legal compliance? Who checks to see what ages their employees are? On the basis of what criteria are those contractors selected? Has the CEO of your company personally attended—unannounced—a safety drill in the Latin American chemical plant? Who, if anybody, reads the pamphlets being distributed about your company by the local opposition party in Kerala? When a community group complains that your construction site's new chief of security used to be the local paramilitary leader, does anyone care? Or check? Many companies can see major improvements just by putting in place the kinds of scanning systems that produce this information—and can produce further learnings from which further improvements will flow.

Continue the Process

Practicing the steps outlined here is part of a learning process that needs investment of time and energy throughout the lifetime of an individual or an organization. Creating a culture in which employees feel encouraged to identify opportunities for improvement requires leadership and courage throughout the company. Implementing and evaluating innovative practices is a time-consuming process in itself. Communicating the company's goals and results clearly to employees and external stakeholders can be a lengthy and often frustrating exercise in dialogue. A company attracts the best, brightest, and most committed employees not as a result of slick recruiting campaigns, but by creating a corporate reputation that makes the best people want to work there. Once the best people are working for the company, they will want to maintain their own self-respect, the company's image, and its reputation by continued improvement and innovation in social as well as business practices—a virtuous circle.

11

Why Good Companies Do Bad Things

This question that we, by implication, began this book with—*why* good companies do bad things—can be partially answered by saying that the world is a complicated place, that none of us can control every feature of our environment, and that, as a result, accidents happen. Unfortunately, the point of our book is that in far too many cases, good companies fail to prevent bad things from happening for the following reasons:

- They fail to create a culture that tolerates dissent or one in which planning processes are encouraged to take nonfinancial risks seriously.
- They focus exclusively on financial measures of performance.
- They discourage employees from thinking about their work as whole people, from using their moral and social intelligence as well as their business intelligence.
- They talk to the same circle of people and information sources all the time and avoid people or organizations who disagree with or criticize them.
- They let their commitment to a particular project or product overwhelm all other considerations—financial, ethical, or social.
- The senior managers consider ethical or social issues as matters for somebody else to resolve—a vice president for social responsibility, the United Nations, the host country government.

In short, when companies have not examined their operations *from a long-term perspective in a social context,* they are much more vulnerable to the type of bad things we have described in this book (what author Ian Mitroff calls crisis-prone companies). We propose that once a company brings this perspective to its strategy development and operational planning, it will, of necessity, reperceive the issue of social responsibility and find many opportunities to turn that issue into a distinctive competency. This process is long term, but its practice is the essence of uniting know-how and integrity. To borrow, again, our friend's metaphor, that deeper long view can be the difference between growing a corporate weed—or a sturdy tree.

Appendix

Given the rapidly increasing number of publications on the subject of corporate social responsibility, we can make no claims for exhaustiveness on behalf of this book. Similarly, many more people have greater expertise than ours in specific fields. This resource list provides a starting point for readers who wish to learn more or to steer their research in a particular direction.

We hope that the suggestions in this book will lead companies to explore other resources (publications and organizations) for further research and action. In addition to those resources listed here, others are contained in the notes section that follows.

Publications

Global Corporate Citizenship—Rationale and Strategies
The Hitachi Foundation
1509 22nd St NW
Washington, DC
USA 20037-1073

We're So Big and Powerful Nothing Bad Can Happen To Us by Ian Mitroff
Carol Publishing
600 Madison Avenue
New York, NY
USA 10022

Worlds Apart—Women and the Global Economy
International Confederation of Free Trade Unions
Blvd Emile Jacmain, 155
B-1210 Brussels
Belgium

Principles for Global Corporate Responsibility
Interfaith Center on Corporate Responsibility
475 Riverside Drive, Room 550
New York, NY
USA 10115-0050

The Better World Investment Guide
Council on Economic Priorities
30 Irving Place
New York, NY 10003

Organizations

Interfaith Center on Corporate Responsibility
475 Riverside Drive, Room 550
New York, NY
USA 10115-0050

The ICCR is a North American association of 275 Protestant, Roman Catholic, and Jewish institutional investors including denominations, religious communities, pension funds, healthcare corporations, dioceses, publishing companies, and foundations with combined portfolios worth an estimated $90 billion.

Business for Social Responsibility
609 Mission Street, Second floor
San Francisco, CA
USA 94105-3506

Business and Social Responsibility provides member companies and others with tools and guidance concerning the development and implementation of policies addressing corporate social responsibility. Examples include providing information on codes of conduct, benchmarking, sourcing audits, specialized information, and facilitating dialogue between the business community and other sectors.

With funding from Levi Strauss and other members, BSR has recently created a Corporate Resource Center on Social Responsibility, which will contain a wide range of resources for interested companies including databases on best practice worldwide and short information summaries on 125 social issues of concern to business.

Business in the Community
44 Baker St
London W1M 1DH
UK

Notes

Preface

xi Developed by attorney Elliot Schrage.

Chapter 1: Social Responsibility in the Context of Globalization

1 Grand Metropolitan, *Report on Corporate Citizenship,* 1997, p. 8.

3 Korten, David, *When Corporations Rule the World,* Kumarian Press, 1995, p. 12.

Chapter 2: Business as a Villain: A Historical Overview

11 Boggia, Raimondo, interview based on book in draft, 1998.

14 From *Capitalism and Slavery* by Eric Williams. Copyright © 1944 by the University of North Carolina Press, renewed (with a new introduction by Colin A. Palmer) 1994. Used by permission of the publisher.

17 Smith, Page, *The Rise of Industrial America,* Penguin, 1990, pp. 478–479.

18 Langley, Lester, and Schoonover, Thomas: *The Banana Men,* University of Kentucky Press, 1995.

19 Minimata website.

20 George, Timothy, Harvard University.

21 *New York Times,* April 29, 1998, p. C5.

21 *The Economist,* June 28, 1997, p. 9.

Chapter 3: Corporations Today

25 Van der Heijden, Kees, Scenarios: *The Art of Strategic Conversation,* Wiley, 1996, Chichester, UK.

26 Material on the Shell case has been drawn from published sources and from conversations between the authors and Shell colleagues or associates over the period before, during, and after the crisis. Coauthor Peter Schwartz was a Shell executive during the 1980s, responsible for corporate planning and the development of the company's innovative scenario planning methodologies.

29 Brummer, Alex, *Guardian,* March 11, 1998.

29 The Shell Report, 1998, p. 39.

31 The following analysis of Brent Spar, Nigeria, and the Shell business idea is based on insights from Kees van der Heijden.

33 *Greenpeace Business,* April/May 1998, p. 2.

33 Material on the Unocal case was drawn from published sources, a personal interview with Unocal's John Imle, and a telephone interview with staff of the Interfaith Center on Corporate Reponsibility.

35 These and succeeding remarks from interview with John Imle, July 30, 1998.

35 Unocal in Myanmar, from a Unocal public document, March 1997, p. 28.

37 U.S. State Department, *1996 Human Rights Report on Burma.*

42 Material on the Nestlé case was drawn entirely from published sources.

44 Material on the Texaco case was drawn from published sources, including Bari-Ellen Roberts's book *Roberts v. Texaco* (Avon Books, 1998) and interviews with Texaco management, including CEO Peter Bijur.

45 These and succeeding remarks from interview with Peter Bijur, August 3, 1998.

46 Nulty, Peter, "Exxon's Problem," *Fortune,* April 23, 1990, p. 204.

47 Report of the Equality and Fairness Task Force, Hon. Deval L. Patrick, Chair, p. 5.

48 Material on the Union Carbide case was taken entirely from published sources.

49 The Union Carbide discussion, especially the five points, draws heavily on Mitroff, Ian, and Linstone Harold, *The Unbounded Mind,* Oxford University Press, 1993, pp. 112–113.

49 Council on Economic Priorities, *Union Carbide: An Executive Summary of the Company's Environmental Policies and Practices,* July 1993.

50 Shrivastava, Paul, *Managing Industrial Crises,* Vision Books, New Delhi, 1992, p. 14.

51 Christian Aid, *The Globe-Trotting Sports Shoe,* 1995. Christian Aid is an international humanitarian NGO based in the United Kingdom.

51 Material on Nike was drawn entirely from published sources, with the exception of some informal conversations with teenage consumers.

52 Christian Aid, *The Globe-Trotting Sports Shoe.*

53 Christian Aid, *The Globe-Trotting Sports Shoe.*

55 Spar, Debora, "The Spotlight and the Bottom Line," *Foreign Affairs,* Vol. 77 No. 2, (March, April 1998) pp. 7–12.

55 Material on A.H. Robins was drawn from published sources and from coauthor Blair Gibb's personal experience. Coauthor Gibb was a claimant in the Dalkon Shield case, unrepresented by an attorney because she was fortunate enough to have complete medical records demonstrating the link between shield-induced infection and her subsequent hysterectomy.

55 Korten, *When Corporations Rule the World,* p. 229.

57 Judge Miles Lord, quoted in Richard Sobol, *Bending the Law,* University of Chicago Press, 1991.

57 Sobol, *Bending the Law,* p. 67.

57 Sixteen years after her original infection, coauthor Gibb received a notice from the court stating that her case had been placed in the category
amounting to the highest level of damage short of death—surgical
sterility—and received a check for $5,500. Four years after that, as if
some cosmic account clerk had been going through old files, she received a second check for $3,000 from the trust fund, with no explana-
tion at all.

58 Punch, Maurice, *Dirty Business,* Sage Publications 1996, p. 165.

58 Warren, Randy, Thalidomide Victims Association, *NYT Magazine,* January 25, 1998 (quote from the FDA Dermatologic and Ophthalmic Drugs
Advisory Committee meeting, September 1997).

59 Warren, Randy, phone interview, May 1998.

60 Material on Bofors was drawn entirely from published sources.

60 Oza, B. M., "Did Rajiv Take the Bofors Bribe," *The Guardian,* Febru-
ary 17, 1997.

61 Material on Thor was drawn entirely from published sources.

61 Hounam, Peter, *Daily Mirror,* 1997.

61 Cameron, James, "Transnational Environmental Disputes," *Asia-Pacific
Journal of Environmental Law,* Vol 1, 1996, p. 12.

62 Television Education Network Program Notes, United Kingdom No-
vember/December 1997, p. 9.

63 Anderson, Kjistine, conversation with author.

63 Coauthor Gibb's most direct experience of this reaction phase took place
immediately following the World Trade Center bombing, when she was
working for the Port Authority of New York, New Jersey, which built
and operated the World Trade Center.

Chapter 4: Risk Management or Scenario Thinking?

70 Van der Heijden, p. 69. Art reproduced by permission.

Chapter 5: Best Practice—and Beyond

75 Stone, Robert, "The High Cost of a Good Drink," *New Yorker Magazine,*
January 26, 1998, p. 6.

78 Lowry, Ritchie, *Good Money: A Guide to Profitable Social Investing in the
90s,* W.W. Norton & Company, 1993.

79 Hawken, Paul, interview, May 12, 1998.

80 Interfaith Center on Corporate Responsibility, *Principles for Global Corporate Responsibility,* 1998, p. 14.

83 Ibid., p. 17.

84 Logan, David, and Laurie Regelbrugge, *Global Corporate Citizenship—
Rationale and Strategies,* The Hitachi Foundation, 1997, p. 16.

84 These quotes are from the unpublished field research notes of Christopher Avery.

90 Ibid.

91   Boele, Richard, interview, September 10, 1998.
92   Levi Strauss & Co., *Communication Guidelines,* 1998.
93   Levi Strauss & Co., *Aspirations Statement,* 1998.
93   Hewlett-Packard internal document, "The HP Way."
93   Conversation with the author.
94   Ibid.

Chapter 6: Reperceiving Social Responsibility

 99   Harald Norvick, Statoil, presentation at Tallberg Workshop, 1998.
103   Art reproduced by permission.
104   Ibid.
105   Quoted by John Kay, *Prospect Magazine,* March 1998, p. 26.
106   Coyote, Peter, letter to GBN, April 15, 1998.
112   Bullock, Alan, *Hitler,* Pelican Books, 1952, p. 199.
114   Conversation with the author.
116   Korten, *When Corporations Rule the World,* p. 229.
119   *Greenpeace Business,* August/September 1998, p. 2.
120   This and other Greenpeace material from interview with Peter Melchett, London, September 15, 1998.
120   Cameron, James, "Transnational Environmental Disputes," p. 5.
120   Porter, Michael B., Class van der Linde, *Green and Competitive: Ends Up the Stalemate,* H.B.R., September 1, 1995.
128   Ikeazor, Chukwudum, interview on August 27, 1998.

**Chapter 7: Business, Governments,
and Nongovernmental Organizations**

132   *Yearbook of International Organizations,* edited by Union of International Organizations, K. G. Saur Verlag, 1998.
132   Fernando, Jude, and Heston, Alan, *Annals of the American Academy of Political and Social Science,* November 1997, p. 8.
142   Thanks to GBN member Gerard Fairtlough for this metaphor.
144   Vargas Llosa, Mario, *A Fish in Water,* Penguin Books, 1995, p. 355.
144   "Managing by Values: Is Levi Strauss Approach Visionary—or Flaky?" *Business Week,* August 1, 1994, pp. 46–52, quoted in Korten, *When Corporations Rule the World,* Kumarian Press, 1995, p. 233.
145   Wheelwright, Jeff, *Degrees of Disaster,* Simon & Schuster, 1994, p. 129.
146   Gail Stewart, e-mail, April 4, 1998.

Chapter 8: Issues of the Future

148   Kolata, Gina, *Clone,* William Morrow & Co., 1998.
150   Davis, Devra Lee, and others, "Reduced Ratio of Male to Female Births in Several Industrial Countries," *Journal of the American Medical Association* Vol. 279, No. 13 (April 1, 1998), pp. 1018–1023; Moller, Henrik, "Trends in sex-ratio, testicular cancer, and male reproductive hazards: Are they connected?" APMIS [Acta Pathologica, Microbiologica et Immunologica Scandinavica] Vol. 106 (1998), pp. 232–239.

152 Shrivavasta, *Managing Industrial Crises,* p. 17.

154 *London Sunday Times,* October 20, 1996, p. 3.

155 Art reproduced by permission.

Chapter 10: Getting Personal

170 In the interests of disclosure, coauthor Schwartz was raised within the Jewish faith and coauthor Gibb in small-town Southern Protestantism. Today, while neither of us could be said to practice a particular religion, our own moral convictions arise from the same place: a belief in the connectedness of human beings to each other, and to the mysteries we see when we look around us. This connectedness is biological, in the sense that we are social animals and hardwired for it as much as bees or wolves are; it is also spiritual, in that the connections we feel to other living things have generated most of the higher impulses humanity has taken pride in through its history. What defines immorality for us, as a result, is the treating of others as instrumentalities only: as "customers," "shareholders," "employees," for example. Social responsibility can only become real if each of us takes *personal* responsibility for those others in the context of the opportunities that life places in front of us to do so.

Index